FOUNDATIONS of DIVINE PROSPERITY

Foundations of Divine Prosperity
ISBN: 978-0-9848710-0-1

Copyright © 2012 by Paul David Cooper

Published by Ariel Publishing, LLC
One Closter Commons,
Closter NJ 07624

The Scripture versions cited in this book are identified in the Appendix, which hereby becomes a part of this copyright page.

All rights reserved. Without limiting the rights under the copyright reserved above, no part of this publication may be reproduced, stored in a retrieval system, or transmitted in any form or by any means—electronic, mechanical, photocopy, recording, or any other—except for brief quotations in printed reviews, without the prior written permission of both the copyright owner and the publisher.

Printed in the United States of America

For Dahlia

And thank you Kenneth.

Table of Contents

Preface xi
Introduction 1

PART 1	MORE THAN MONEY 5
Chapter 1	An Apostolic View of Prosperity: John's Prayer 7
Chapter 2	Prosperity is More Than Money 9
	A Working Definition of Prosperity 9
	Prosperity Includes Physical Healing 12
Chapter 3	Prosperity and the Soul 17
	Biblical Meditation 21
	The Benefits of Biblical Meditation 31
	An Example of Meditation 35
	Failing to Meditate Means Failing to Prosper 37
	Train Yourself to Meditate 37
Chapter 4	Divine Prosperity Includes Money 39

PART 2	PROSPERITY IN THE BEGINNING 41
Chapter 5	Man was Made to Prosper 43
	In His Image and Likeness 44
	Purpose and Prosperity 45

	The Earth was Designed for Prosperity 48	
	Man's Terrestrial Source of Prosperity 49	
PART 3	**PROSPERITY AND REDEMPTION** **51**	
Chapter 6	Man's Fall from Prosperity 53	
Chapter 7	God's Recovery Plan 61	
	What is Redemption? 61	
	The Three Clues of Redemption 62	
	The Redemptive Mystery 65	
Chapter 8	Abraham's Inheritance 69	
	Abraham's Inheritance is Spiritual 73	
	The Material Aspects of Abraham's Inheritance 74	
	Abraham's Inheritance is for His Descendants 75	
	Abraham's Inheritance is for National Israel 78	
	The Blessing and the Law 80	
	Abraham's Inheritance is for the Church 82	
PART 4	**THE PROSPERITY OF OUR INHERITANCE IN CHRIST** **87**	
Chapter 9	Forgiveness of Sins 89	
	Bound by Sin 91	
	The Curse of the Law 93	
	The Curse of the Law is a Judgment from God 95	
	Redeemed from Sin by Jesus Christ 97	
	Set Free from Sin but Not Exempt from Suffering 101	
Chapter 10	Deliverance from Satan's Power 103	
	The Cross of Christ Destroyed Satan's Power 105	
	Christ and the Church are Exalted Far Above Satan 107	

Table of Contents

	Satan Still Rages Against the Church	108
	Satan the Thief	109
Chapter 11	The Superiority of Our Inheritance	117
	The Spirit and the Natural	119
	The Interaction of the Spirit and the Natural	121
	The Superiority of the Spirit Over the Natural	123
Chapter 12	The Authority of Our Inheritance	125
	Our Inheritance Includes the Power of God	128
PART 5	**CONTRASTING DIVINE WEALTH AND WORLDLY WEALTH**	**131**
Chapter 13	Defining Divine Wealth	133
	Divine Prosperity to Meet Our Needs	135
	Wealth to Preach the Gospel	137
	God's Work Requires Money	137
	Old Testament Examples of Financing God's Work	139
	New Testament Examples of Financing God's Work	144
Chapter 14	Worldly Prosperity	149
	Honest Labor as Opposed to Worldly Prosperity	151
	The World's System is Not the Church's System	152
Chapter 15	Understanding Greed	157
Chapter 16	Portraits of Greed	163
	A Conversation Between Two Rich Men	164
	Achan and the Misery of Greed	166
	The Intemperance of Gehazi	169
	The Prosperity of Our Portion	171
	The Prosperity of Restraint	174

Chapter 17	Biblical Ways to Overcome Greed	177
	Do Not Be Haughty	*177*
	Give	*178*
	Be Content	*179*

PART 6 PROSPERITY AND SUFFERING 183

Chapter 18	The Mystery of Suffering	185
Chapter 19	Suffering for Sin	189
	Suffering as a Consequence of Our Sins	*193*
	Suffering Because of God's Chastisement	*194*
Chapter 20	Suffering Because the World is Fallen	199
Chapter 21	Suffering Because of Delays	203
Chapter 22	Suffering for the Sake of Righteousness	207
	A Multifaceted Concept	*208*
	Allowed by God, Not Caused by God	*209*
	Suffering is Part of God's Prosperity Plan	*210*
Chapter 23	The Mystery of Christ's Suffering	213
Chapter 24	Suffering Due to Satanic Affliction	217
Chapter 25	Reconciling Prosperity and Suffering	219
	Rich and Poor Are Relative Concepts	*219*
	In the Light of Divine Prosperity, Why Was Jesus Poor?	*220*
	In the Light of Divine Prosperity, Why Were the Apostles Poor?	*223*
	In the Light of Divine Prosperity, Why Was the Early Church Poor?	*227*
Chapter 26	Summary on Suffering	231

Table of Contents

PART 7   **PROSPERITY IS CONDITIONAL** **235**

Chapter 27   Preconditions of Prosperity 237
                       The Necessity of Faith *237*
                       Prosperity is a Lifestyle *240*

PART 8   **EPILOGUE** **243**

Chapter 28   Super Prosperity 245

PART 9   **APPENDIX** **249**
                       Use of Bible Versions 251
                       Bible References 251
                       Copyright Information 253
                       Works Cited 255
                       End Notes 257

Preface

THIS BOOK IS WRITTEN for believers seeking instruction in the principles of divine prosperity. It is my prayer that as you continue to abide in Christ and grow in his grace, the Lord will use this book to reveal truths about finances that you can put into practice immediately. The harvest is abundant, and it will take a large company of dedicated and informed believers to finance the preaching of the Gospel to all nations. Therefore, this book focuses on establishing a solid foundation of doctrine about divine prosperity, rather than proposing a spiritual mishmash of fanciful schemes for getting rich quickly.

Because this book is primarily written for Christians, if you are not a believer, then you will likely find this book perplexing. I encourage you to make Jesus Christ the Lord of your life, because salvation in Christ is the starting point for all forms of true prosperity.

I pray that you prosper and be in good health, even as your soul prospers.

Paul David Cooper
Closter, NJ

Introduction: The Case for Prosperity

PROSPERITY IS A CONTROVERSIAL and vexing issue in the Body of Christ. Many believers are confused by the swirl of teachings and alarmed by the acrimonious exchanges between leaders on the subject. These feuds have left many believers in a difficult position. On the one hand, believers intuitively know that they need finances to function and that they have a responsibility to be good stewards of their money. On the other hand, they want to avoid being materialistic or covetous, or seeming that way, by openly embracing biblical promises about money.

Christians need to dialogue freely about money with the understanding that, although controversies may erupt in the Church for many reasons, controversy itself is no indication that a particular doctrine is wrong or harmful.

The Lord has revived many doctrines that some have found controversial. For example, so-called Church leaders resisted the apostle Paul's doctrine of grace because they believed that one first had to convert to Judaism to be saved. False teachers also distorted the doctrine of grace as a license to sin. Similarly, some find the teaching that God prospers his people controversial and some have abused it. However, neither the controversy nor the abuse can change the biblical basis for prosperity.

Communication also is an important consideration in the prosperity debate. Church groups teach prosperity differently and communicate about prosperity in unique ways. The Word of Faith movement, for example, has a distinctive way of presenting prosperity teaching that often is opaque to other religious groups and makes the common ground harder to recognize. In writing this book, I attempt to present doctrinal concepts clearly and plainly to avoid confusion.

Certainly, Christian leaders disagree. It is not a case of attributing the errors of a few to the many, or misunderstanding a doctrinal position or unclear language. It is a matter of understanding a position and concluding that it is false. Sometimes these disagreements are reasonable and cordial, but often they are acrimonious and, in extreme cases, violent. Again, a study of Church history reveals that many orthodox beliefs were once hotly disputed by Church leaders, including salvation by faith alone, the Resurrection, the Incarnation, and the return of Christ.

With prosperity teaching, it is common for Christian teachers to disagree on theological grounds. Further complicating the matter is that no single group owns or propagates the *prosperity message*, as nearly all Christian groups believe in material prosperity to some degree. However, although the religious conflict on prosperity has led to bitter divisions, honest debate, when allowed, has led to change on all sides. For example, prosperity teaching in a Charismatic context has evolved. Ministers have

Introduction

refined their messages and become more careful, precise, and thoughtful in how they present their point of view to a global audience who may be unfamiliar with their theology. In a wider Evangelical context, there seems a realization that one cannot maintain a disdain for teaching on money in church and be effective in raising finances for ministry projects. It takes money to preach the Gospel using every medium possible, and if God's people do not prosper, they will not have money to fund Gospel projects.

Why You Need to Prosper

Although Church leaders disagree over the prosperity message, Christians should not get flustered by this and stop seeking the truth in this area. It is best to exercise discretion by evaluating a position in the light of Scripture and come to your own conclusions. Furthermore, the practical side of money in the Christian life cannot be denied. If you are struggling financially and concerned about how you are going to meet your financial obligations, then you need to prosper. If you desire to support Christian relief work, contribute to the building program at your church, or help the poor, then you need to prosper. For you to prosper, you will have to study what the Scriptures say about divine prosperity, develop faith in God's promises, and learn how to pray for prosperity confidently. If you are filled with negativity and doubt about the idea of God making you prosperous, then you will not see victory in this area.

My prayer is that this book will help you establish a foundation for manifesting divine prosperity in your life.

PART 1
MORE THAN MONEY

An Apostolic View of Prosperity: John's Prayer

¹ The Elder,
To the beloved Gaius, whom I love in truth:

² Beloved, **I pray that you may prosper in all things and be in health, just as your soul prospers.**

³ For I rejoiced greatly when brethren came and testified of the truth that is in you, just as you walk in the truth.

⁴ I have no greater joy than to hear that my children walk in truth.

3 John 1:1-4 (NKJV)

SOME MAY FIND IT SURPRISING that the apostle John actually prayed for prosperity and healing.[1] Most theologians agree that this same John walked and talked with Jesus and wrote the Gospel of John. John was now an elderly man, with many years of fruitful service to the Lord. He oversaw several churches in Asia and wrote letters to them.

The apostle John undoubtedly knew the will of God, and knew how to pray. Therefore, it is significant that he prayed specifically for prosperity and healing. John was praying for a church leader named Gaius, and was commending Gaius for his faithfulness in receiving and supporting traveling ministers who had been sent out to proclaim the Gospel:

> [5] Beloved, you do faithfully whatever you do for the brethren and for strangers,
>
> [6] who have borne witness of your love before the church. If you send them forward on their journey in a manner worthy of God, you will do well,
>
> [7] because they went forth for His name's sake, taking nothing from the Gentiles.
>
> 3 John 1:5–7 (NKJV)

Gaius worked hard to serve the church and to be a blessing. Perhaps, he had reached a point of exhaustion in his ministry and he felt discouraged. He might have been ill and perhaps even suffering financially. John was praying that Gaius would be prosperous in every way so he could continue his ministry.

John's letter to Gaius is our starting point for helping us understand the scriptural view of prosperity. John's view may be summarized in three points:

- Prosperity is more than money.
- Prosperity begins in the soul.
- Prosperity includes money.

Prosperity is More Than Money

ALTHOUGH THE WORD *PROSPERITY* is often associated with money and material things, we can see from John's phrase "prosper in all things" that biblical prosperity is not merely being blessed with material things. Biblical or divine prosperity refers to the prosperity that comes from God, in contrast to the prosperity that comes from the world. To have divine prosperity means to be blessed in every aspect of our lives, whether spiritual, mental, or physical.

The focus of this book is the financial aspect of divine prosperity. Although finance is not the most important feature of divine prosperity, it is perhaps one of the most neglected and misunderstood. Even so, it is crucial to establish that divine prosperity is far more than financial or material blessing.

A Working Definition of Prosperity

The word *prosperity* means *well-being*. According to W.E. Vine's *Expository Dictionary of New Testament Words,* the Greek word used in this verse literally means to be "helped on one's way" and connotes "physical and spiritual health," as well as "to cause to prosper" and "to be successful."[2] The Merriam-Webster Collegiate Dictionary defines prosperity as "the condition of being successful or thriving; especially: economic well-being."[3]

Biblical prosperity is beyond money and refers to man's ultimate spiritual condition. Salvation through Christ is both the beginning and the ultimate state of prosperity. The greatest act that could ever happen to any person is to have their sins washed away by the blood of Jesus and be transferred from the kingdom of darkness into the kingdom of his dear Son. When we are born again, God makes us prosperous in a way that will take all of eternity to comprehend (Ephesians 2:7). Truly, God's salvation in Christ is the highest form of prosperity.

To speak of redemption as a form of prosperity is consistent with Scripture. In fact, the Apostles used language that is normally associated with financial prosperity to describe our salvation in Christ:

- Our salvation is called "an inheritance," planned before the foundation of the world, and predestined according to the kind intention of God's will (Ephesians 1:1–14, Colossians 1:12).
- The believer has been blessed with "every spiritual blessing in the heavenly places" (Ephesians 1:3 ESV).
- Our redemption was provided to us "according to the riches of his grace, which the Father lavished upon us, in all wisdom and insight" (Ephesians 1:7–8 ESV).

- The believer needs supernatural insight to grasp the riches of God's "glorious inheritance in the saints" (Ephesians 1:18 ESV).

- The Father has provided an "immeasurably great," "surpassingly great," and "incomparably great" power for us who believe, to aid us in living to the praise of his glory (Ephesians 1:14–23 various translations). This "mighty power" was given to God's people out of the "rich treasury of His glory" for their strength and reinforcement (Ephesians 3:16 Amplified).

- Although we were "children of wrath," God redeemed us because of his "great love for us" and because he is "rich in mercy" (Ephesians 2:3–4 ESV).

- God's intention is to show us "through the ages to come the immeasurable (limitless, surpassing) riches of His free grace (His unmerited favor) in [His] kindness and goodness of heart toward us in Christ Jesus" (Ephesians 2:7 Amplified).

- The Gospel that the apostle Paul proclaimed is called the "unending (boundless, fathomless, incalculable, and exhaustless) riches of Christ [wealth which no human being could have searched out]," (Ephesians 3:8 Amplified).

- In Christ, all the fullness of the Deity lives in bodily form. The believer receives Christ's fullness and is made complete in Christ (Colossians 2:9–10), and has been given all things (1 Corinthians 3:21).

Words like *inheritance, lavish, riches, immeasurable, surpassing, treasury,* and *fullness* are **prosperity words,** and they are words that God the Holy Spirit used to describe our spiritual inheritance in Christ. Given these Scriptures, and the many others like them in the Bible, we easily conclude that **everything** about our salvation is rich, abundant, and prosperous.

In the light of these great truths of redemption, when believers hear the word *prosperity* in a sermon or Christian conversation, we do not have to become wary. For the Church, prosperity is **our** word. We understand well-being at a level known only to those who have been redeemed by Christ. Prosperity is hardwired into our salvation. We can boldly declare that we are a prosperous people in Christ!

Prosperity Includes Physical Healing

John's prayer that Gaius would be in good health reveals that the Holy Spirit inspired John to emphasize that healing is a form of prosperity, and to pray for Gaius to be healthy. (The Holy Spirit would not have led John to pray for good health if it were not God's will.) I am not suggesting that people who are in bad health are spiritually inferior or necessarily experiencing God's disfavor. Gaius was clearly a beloved and faithful Christian, and perhaps he was ill. If, indeed he was, then the apostle John did not get defensive about Gaius' illness. His prayer was simple: that Gaius should be in good health.

Usually, we are most effective when we are in good health and feeling well. Most unwell Christians desire to be well, in part because they want to resume their lives and ministries as before. Of course, I am not saying that believers cannot be effective if they are not in good health. However, these exceptions should not become a doctrinal stance. We, however, can derive a doctrinal position from Scripture. The apostle Peter wrote:

> [24] He himself bore our sins in his body on the tree, that we might die to sin and live to righteousness. **By his wounds you have been healed.**
>
> [25] For you were straying like sheep, but have now returned to the Shepherd and Overseer of your souls.
>
> 1 Peter 2:24-25 (ESV)

The Apostles taught that healing was part of Christ's redemptive work. When Christ was crucified, he not only bore our sins, but also bore our sicknesses (physical ailments). Indeed, the Apostles interpreted the earthly ministry of Jesus as a fulfillment of the prophecy that the Savior would be the healer of his people:

> [4] Surely he has borne our griefs and carried our sorrows; yet we esteemed him stricken, smitten by God, and afflicted.
>
> [5] But he was wounded for our transgressions; he was crushed for our iniquities; upon him was the chastisement that brought us peace, and with his stripes we are healed.

> ⁶ All we like sheep have gone astray; we have turned—every one—to his own way; and the LORD has laid on him the iniquity of us all.
>
> Isaiah 53:4–6 (ESV)

The Amplified Bible brings out the additional meaning of the word *griefs* in the original language:

> ⁴ Surely He has borne our griefs (**sicknesses, weaknesses, and distresses**) and carried our sorrows and pains [of punishment], yet we [ignorantly] considered Him stricken, smitten, and afflicted by God [as if with leprosy].
>
> Isaiah 53:4 (Amplified)

Isaiah is prophesying about Christ's redemptive work. He bore our sins and griefs (our sicknesses, weaknesses and distresses), accomplishing not only the forgiveness of our sins but also physical healing for our minds and bodies. This physical healing is part of the believer's inheritance in Christ. This understanding of Isaiah's witness is confirmed in Matthew's Gospel:

> ¹⁴ And when Jesus entered Peter's house, he saw his mother-in-law lying sick with a fever.
>
> ¹⁵ He touched her hand, and the fever left her, and she rose and began to serve him.
>
> ¹⁶ That evening they brought to him many who were oppressed by demons, and he cast out the spirits with a word and healed all who were sick.
>
> ¹⁷ This was to fulfill what was spoken by the prophet Isaiah: "**He took our illnesses and bore our diseases.**"
>
> Matthew 8:14–17 (ESV)

Peter's mother-in-law was physically sick, and Christ healed her. Later in the day, Jesus went on to heal the sick and drive out demons. This activity of physical healing and exorcism fulfilled what Isaiah foretold. Healing was so central to Christ's ministry that Peter summed up Christ's work in this way:

> ³⁸ how God anointed Jesus of Nazareth with the Holy Spirit and with power. He went about **doing good and healing** all who were oppressed by the devil, for God was with him.
>
> Acts 10:38 (ESV)

Note that healing was classified with "doing good." Healing is a **good thing** and is a form of prosperity. The early Church had no doubts whether healing from Christ belonged to them, because healing was part of the Gospel message that the Apostles passed on to them. Divine healing is not an obscure doctrine that God has relegated to the Christian backburner. It is not an improbable hope that appeals to the poor, the uneducated, or the unsophisticated. Divine healing, manifesting as a cure for diseases and ailments, is woven into the fabric of our spiritual inheritance in Christ.

It was God's idea to provide to the Church not only the forgiveness of sins, but also physical healing for our bodies. Despite the objections of some, the Scripture will not change:

> ² Beloved, I pray that you may prosper in all things and be in health, just as your soul prospers.
>
> 3 John 1:2 (NKJV)

Divine prosperity includes divine health!

Prosperity and the Soul

THE APOSTLE JOHN TAUGHT that prosperity begins in the soul and that believers will prosper and be in health to the degree that their souls prosper. John's reference to the soul is deliberate. The human soul is the gateway to manifesting divine prosperity, and the condition of the human soul determines how divine prosperity is manifested in a believer's life. Although we might assume that *spirit* and *soul* mean the same thing, the Word of God divides them:

> [12] For the word of God is living and active, sharper than any two-edged sword, piercing **to the division of soul and of spirit**, of joints and of marrow, and discerning the thoughts and intentions of the heart.
>
> Hebrews 4:12 (ESV)

Spirit and *soul* are different words in Greek, and although they are close in meaning, they do not mean the same thing.[4] Essentially, man consists of three parts:

- The human spirit: the inward part of man re-created by God in the new birth.

- The human soul: the seat of man's intellect, will, and emotions. The human soul is distinct from the human spirit, but also inseparable.[5] The key distinction for the purposes of this discussion is that the new birth did not re-create the human soul (that is, our mind, will, and emotions).

- The human body: the physical part of our being which houses the spirit and soul. When the human body perishes, the human spirit and soul inseparably live on. The human body was not re-created in the new birth; however, all believers will receive a glorified body when the Lord returns.

Dr. Kenneth E. Hagin's teaching on spirit, soul, and body presents this complex truth in an accessible way. In his writings,[6] he explains that our *spirit man* was regenerated in the new birth. Our spirit man is the real you and I, and is called the "hidden man of the heart" (1 Peter 3:4). As a spirit being, we have a soul, which is our intellect, will, and emotions. The human soul is also an invisible part of our nature, and is essentially inseparable from our human spirit, but as noted, is not regenerated in the new birth. This is why, when we received Christ, we retained the same intellect, will, and emotions.

Besides having a soul, our *spirit man* lives in a body. The body is our connection to this earth realm, and when our bodies die, the spirit and soul continue. When we received Christ, the body was not regenerated. Paraphrasing Dr. Hagin, if we were bald **before** we were saved, we are still bald **after** we were saved. Although people may be tremendously touched in their soul and body when they receive Christ, the human soul and body are not **re-created** in the new birth. However, when the human spirit is reborn in Christ, the human spirit is re-created, not renovated. In short, God creates a **new you.** The old you was a slave to sin. The new you is the righteousness of God and is instantly aligned with God. The new you, your spirit man, wants exactly what God wants, and has unhindered access to God. However, both the soul and body have catching up to do. The soul is still carnal and must be renewed by hearing the Word of God. The mind and emotions of a person have to be trained to think like God and to respond like God. The body still wants to live the way it has been living, and it too has to be trained to act in a godly way. **The struggle that all re-created Christians have to endure is to rein in their minds and bodies, and to learn how to live godly lives in an ungodly world.**

The struggle is worth it. John teaches that once we can get our minds to act in line with the Word of God, then we can start experiencing God's best manifestation of divine prosperity in our lives. (Although 3 John 2 does not directly mention the body, controlling the mind leads to controlling the body; for example, see Romans 12:1–2.)

The necessary qualifier for reining in our bodies is one reason that some people do not get results from prosperity teaching. People approach the *prosperity message* thinking that it works by some kind of unsophisticated formula. They neglect to consider that they have to bring their thoughts and actions in alignment to the Word of God, and that crucifying the flesh is not a quick or easy process.

My sister-in-law and her husband had a large dog, Deezy, which they kept chained to a porch rail. I was fond of the dog, and once, during a visit, I took him for a walk. Deezy was so happy to get some exercise that he nearly pulled me down the street! When we came to a large field, Deezy spotted another dog, happily playing off his leash. On seeing this other dog, Deezy went wild. He wanted to run and play with that other dog, and controlling him was hard.

Likewise, controlling our minds, our emotions, and our bodies can be extremely difficult. We have to fill our minds with Scripture so we will reason from a biblical point of view. We have to meditate on the Word of God, so when problems come, we will react out of faith and not fear. In addition, we have to put into practice the truths of Scripture, so by constant use, we will learn how to walk in holiness.

The apostle John is teaching us that God wants our souls to prosper, and that our general state of prosperity and good health is directly tied to the degree in which our souls are prospering. Because God wants our souls to prosper, he wants our **intellects** to develop and become productive, our **wills** to become strong and steady, and his Word to govern our **emotions.**

Biblical Meditation

Christians have an innate thirst for knowledge. Christian groups are constantly forming schools, publishing educational materials, and promoting activities that increase enlightenment and understanding. Because people who pursue God will pursue knowledge in all arenas that might be used for the glory of God. For example, studying God will awaken a thirst for justice and righteousness in society. Studying God also will nurture a natural curiosity for the universe that he created, and, therefore, lead to an interest in science and physical laws. Adoration of God will cultivate an appreciation for the arts. Because of a love for God and his laws, Christians have been inspired to make significant contributions in the realms of science, literature, the arts, law, and government. This is why believers founded and funded many great universities in the West. However, despite this proud tradition of academic excellence, some Christian groups have become suspicious of secular education. Education in a worldly environment can be spiritually corrosive, and even in the finest universities, there may be an attitude of hostility and derision toward anything Christian. However, that is not a problem with education; it is a problem with the educators. Christians should not flee academe because a college professor publishes a book promoting atheism. Believers are salt and light in this world, and are called to demonstrate to the world that God will always confirm his Word.

Some of the most impressive men of Scripture were highly educated and trained in a secular system. Moses was trained in the courts of Pharaoh. Joseph also learned how to flourish in the Egyptian government. Daniel was educated in the ways of the Babylonians. These men learned the protocol, the arts, the sciences and the literature of secular society, and God used them to dominate in their arenas. Moses was the master of Pharaoh and his wise men. Joseph was indispensable to all of Egypt. Daniel was a prominent and important leader in Babylon and became a ruler of the order of magicians (Magi). In our endeavor to study the Bible, we should not neglect other areas of learning. A truly prosperous Church will be an educated Church.

Education should be applied, and, therefore, labor and vocation are important aspects of prosperity. God expects us to develop ourselves intellectually and use our skills to earn income.

Education is not limited to going to school and earning a degree. Education should be a lifelong pursuit of becoming smarter about important and positive subjects. For example, there is much good and common sense information that believers need to know about managing debt, savings, and investments. Many times, Christians become poor because they have not learned about financial management.

Although the pursuit of knowledge and learning may take us down various paths of study and work, embracing Scripture is fundamental in developing the soul and transforming our will and emotions. When John writes that he prays for us to prosper as our soul prospers, he is echoing what God spoke to Joshua:

> ⁸ This Book of the Law shall not depart from your mouth, but you shall meditate on it day and night, so that you may be careful to do according to all that is written in it. For then you will make your way prosperous, and then you will have good success.
>
> Joshua 1:8 (ESV)

In this passage, God revealed to Joshua how to be prosperous and successful. God told Joshua that prosperity would come by meditating constantly on the Word of God ("Book of the Law" equals the Word of God). In turn, this would allow Joshua to obey the Word diligently. The New King James translates Joshua 1:8 this way:

> ⁸ This Book of the Law shall not depart from your mouth, but you shall meditate in it day and night, that you may **observe to do** according to all that is written in it. For then you will make your way prosperous, and then you will have good success.

It is one thing to **do** a command, and another to **observe to do** a command. It is one thing for a child to do her chores, and a different thing for a child first to consider the work that needs to be done, then to do it with the utmost diligence. Businesses all over the world are looking for attentive and diligent people, because these kinds of workers will help their business prosper. God is telling Joshua that when we become diligent about obeying his Word, we will prosper and be successful.

When we meditate on Scripture, our minds become enlightened to God's desire for our lives. God's desire will become our desire and our conviction. The more we meditate on the Word, the stronger our conviction about the Word will become. Soon, our conviction will drive our behavior. Eventually, we will experience a manifestation of the Word of God in our lives. That is the power of biblical meditation.

Meditation Involves Speaking

What is meditation? The word *meditate* does not mean to clear one's mind to achieve an altered state. In Hebrew, the word means to *mutter*, *imagine*, or *muse*.[7] It means to contemplate and speak the Word to oneself to get the Word deep within you. In Joshua, we see the connection between meditation and speaking when the Scripture says, "do not let this Book of the Law depart from your mouth." This reference to speaking the Word is found elsewhere in Scripture. The Psalmist wrote:

> [28] And my tongue shall speak of thy righteousness and of thy praise all the day long.
>
> Psalms 35:28 (KJV)

The word "speak" in this verse is the same word that is translated as "meditate" in Joshua 1:8. Although biblical meditation involves speaking, it is not mindless repetition or chanting–it is the speaking that accompanies reflection or pondering of a subject.

This kind of meditation should be readily familiar to most of us. For example, in any school, some students seek only to get by, learning just enough information to repeat it for a test. Although they have memorized the material, what they have learned has not become a part of them. Shortly after the course has finished, they forget most of what they have memorized. Then there are students who want to understand the material, not just memorize it to pass a test. Their study involves thinking deeply about the subject and going over it in their minds. Perhaps they participate in study groups where they excitedly discuss what they are learning with their peers. In their enthusiasm for the subject, they will talk through the concepts they are studying. This kind of learning is meditation, and results in a successful educational outcome.

The notion of learning by speaking is also presented in the book of Deuteronomy:

> ⁶ And these words which I am commanding you this day shall be [first] in your [own] minds and hearts; [then]
>
> ⁷ You shall whet and sharpen them so as to make them penetrate, and teach and impress them diligently upon the [minds and] hearts of your children, **and shall talk of them** when you sit in your house and when you walk by the way, and when you lie down and when you rise up.
>
> Deuteronomy 6:6–7 (Amplified)

The Amplified Bible uses interesting imagery here. Speaking God's Word to your children is like "whetting and sharpening" a sword that would penetrate their hearts and minds. God commanded parents to train their children how to meditate so they would know how to keep God's laws.

Meditating on Scripture is like a cow chewing cud. The cow grazes, eating all the grass it wants. Then, when it is full, it settles down in a field, perhaps under a tree, and brings up the grass it has eaten (namely, the cud) and chews it repeatedly, further digesting it. In doing this, the cow gets maximum nutritional benefit from the grass.

As Christians, we go to church and hear the Word preached. We further study the Scripture on our own, through personal Bible study or listening to recorded sermons. That is the process of hearing and studying. Meditation is the part when we reflect deeply on what we have heard and studied. For instance, we can meditate on a scriptural phrase, such as, "the just shall live by faith." We turn that phrase repeatedly in our minds, repeating it to ourselves, thinking about the meaning of that Scripture. Perhaps we discuss this passage with our spouse or with our friends at church. The more God's Word is reflected on, spoken, discussed, and confessed, then the stronger it becomes in our hearts. Because God created humanity (and all of creation) to respond to the spoken Word, hearing Scripture, particularly out of our own mouths, has an extraordinary impact upon our entire being (spirit, soul, and body). For the soul, hearing the Word brings revelation to our minds. With our spirit and soul thus enlightened, we can begin to train our bodies to do the will of God. The apostle Paul writes about this transformation in the book of Romans:

> ¹ I appeal to you therefore, brothers, by the mercies of God, to present your bodies as a living sacrifice, holy and acceptable to God, which is your spiritual worship.
>
> ² Do not be conformed to this world, but be transformed by the renewal of your mind, that by testing you may discern what is the will of God, what is good and acceptable and perfect.
>
> Romans 12:1-2 (ESV)

Biblical meditation is a new way of thinking, not clearing the mind, instead filling our minds and our mouths with Scripture.

Meditation Involves Passionate Delight

The book of Psalms records an added dimension to meditation that we should consider:

> ¹ Blessed is the man who walks not in the counsel of the wicked, nor stands in the way of sinners, nor sits in the seat of scoffers;
>
> ² but his **delight** is in the law of the LORD, and on his law he meditates day and night.
>
> ³ He is like a tree planted by streams of water that yields its fruit in its season, and its leaf does not wither. In all that he does, he prospers.
>
> Psalms 1:1-3 (ESV)

To be productive in meditating on Scripture, one has to delight in Scripture. There has to be a strong desire, a passion, even a yearning for the truth of Scripture. Consider the following excerpts from Psalm 119:

> ⁴⁷ for I find my delight in your commandments, **which I love**
>
> ⁴⁸ I will lift up my hands toward your commandments, **which I love**, and I will meditate on your statutes.
>
> ⁹⁷ **Oh how I love** your law! It is my meditation all the day.
>
> Psalms 119:47–48, 97 (ESV)

Delighting in God's commandments means that we put the Word first in our lives. It means that above all else, we give heed to the Word so we will obey it. It means that pursuit and obedience of God's commandments is more important than the pursuit of money. This kind of passion is essential to being effective in meditation, and this is the kind of passion often seen in the world. For example, when I had a long work commute, I enjoyed listening to sports radio. It was interesting to listen to several people calling to openly speak about the sports issues of the day. One show in particular was fun to listen to because, as the hosts and callers discussed and debated an issue, they considered every statistic and subtle fact about a player or team. What was so compelling about the show was the sheer satisfaction the hosts and callers had reveling in the details of sports. That is the enthusiasm, energy, and dedication that believers should have for Scripture. Believers should be in the Word of God with at least as much gusto and seriousness that a sports fan has for his or her team.

Like speaking the Word, delighting in the Word is an essential part of biblical meditation. You can quote Scriptures until you are blue in the face, but if you neither believe nor delight in the Word that you are saying, it will have no impact on your life.

The one who delights in the Word will abide in the Word:

> [4] Abide in Me, and I in you. As the branch cannot bear fruit of itself, unless it abides in the vine, neither can you, unless you abide in Me.
>
> [5] "I am the vine, you are the branches. He who abides in Me, and I in him, bears much fruit; for without Me you can do nothing.
>
> [7] "If you abide in Me, and My words abide in you, you will ask what you desire, and it shall be done for you.
>
> John 15:4-5, 7 (NKJV)

In this verse, Jesus affirms the link between prosperity and meditation. The prosperity part of this verse is, "you will ask what you desire, and it shall be done for you." The meditation part of this verse is, "abide in Me, and My words abide in you." Jesus is reiterating the same concept stated in Joshua 1 and Psalms 1. If we meditate on the Word of God and are careful to do it, then we will prosper in everything we do.

MEDITATION INVOLVES IMAGINATION

Meditate has been translated *imagine*. According to the dictionary, the word *imagine* means "to form a mental image of (something not present)."[8] Often, when Christians hear words like *visualization* and *imagination*, they associate it with some type of non-Christian mysticism. However, as believers, we may employ our imaginations as a tool for our spiritual progress. We are not to imagine just anything, but to imagine the promises of God manifesting in our lives.

God has always stirred man's imagination. For example, God told Abraham that his descendants would be "as numerous as the stars in the heavens and the grains of sand on the seashore" (Genesis 22:17). That tremendous description certainly engaged Abraham's imagination. Moses' vivid description of the Promised Land of Israel is another example of how God intended his people to visualize their blessing:

> [7] For the Lord your God is bringing you into a good land, a land of brooks of water, of fountains and springs, flowing out in the valleys and hills,
>
> [8] a land of wheat and barley, of vines and fig trees and pomegranates, a land of olive trees and honey,
>
> [9] a land in which you will eat bread without scarcity, in which you will lack nothing, a land whose stones are iron, and out of whose hills you can dig copper.
>
> Deuteronomy 8:7–9 (ESV)

These verses are *poverty killer* verses. After reading Scripture like this, it is difficult to believe that God wants his people to be broke and penniless. Meditating on this verse is to see a lush, abundant land teeming with food and provision in our mind's eye, and to understand this is God's will for his people.

The Benefits of Biblical Meditation

Because divine prosperity is more than money, the success and prosperity that comes from biblical meditation is more than financial. Wonderful benefits come from biblical meditation.

MEDITATION DEVELOPS FAITH

First, meditation on the Scripture develops faith. As we meditate on Scripture, we are literally soaking our spirit and mind with the Word of God. At a certain point, the Scriptures we are meditating on begin to register in our inner man. We begin to **hear** what the Lord is saying. This is not as mysterious as it may sound. If you have ever studied a foreign language, for example, there comes a time, after consistent study and practice that the language begins to click. Your mind and mouth work together, and the phrases roll out of you. Similarly, there comes a point when the Word of God takes root in our hearts and we develop a **conviction**. At this point, the Scripture is primed to bear fruit: thirty, sixty, or hundredfold (Matthew 13:23). What kind of fruit does it produce? The kind of seed sown in the heart first; that is, the fruit reflects the content of the Scripture being pondered.

Therefore, if you meditate on Scriptures about the Holy Spirit, the fruit of that meditation will be a deeper relationship with the Holy Spirit and a greater understanding of his work in your life. If you meditate on Scriptures about the believer's victory over fear, the fruit of that meditation will be a strong faith to stand against fear attacks from the enemy. Moreover, if you meditate on Scriptures that promise you financial prosperity, the fruit in your life will be a strong faith to receive and manifest financial blessing.

This process does not happen overnight. Nevertheless, it is worth the wait and the effort, because operating in faith is necessary to receive anything from God by intention. (By his sovereign will, God can give us anything without our faith, but that is according to his intention, not ours.) The Lord told Joshua that if he meditated on the Word, whatever he did would prosper. That is prosperity by intention.

MEDITATION DEVELOPS BALANCE

Second, meditation on Scripture develops balance. To meditate properly on a portion of Scripture, we have to seek understanding about **all** of Scripture. For example, the apostle Paul wrote to the Philippian church:

> [19] And my God will supply every need of yours according to his riches in glory in Christ Jesus.
>
> Philippians 4:19 (ESV)

This wonderful promise has comforted millions over the ages. Any believer could spend weeks and months chewing the cud of this Scripture. However, you cannot extract all the insight into that Scripture unless you read not only all of Philippians 4, but also the entire letter to the Philippians. Reading the account in Acts where Paul went to Philippi would be helpful too. However, do not stop there; why not read the whole book of Acts? And on it goes.

Again, I am not saying that you have to read the entire Bible before you could start believing Philippians 4:19 to get your needs met. However, the more Scripture you meditate, the more clarity you will have about Philippians 4:19. Moreover, the greater your clarity, the stronger your faith will become. The stronger your faith, the more evident the fruit of faith will be in your life.

Meditation Is a Hedge Against Covetousness

The recurring criticism of biblical teaching on financial prosperity is that such teaching promotes greed. That criticism contains a valid concern in that it recognizes that covetousness is toxic to the life of the believer and that any teaching that encourages such attitudes should be forthrightly condemned. However, the criticism is invalid to the extent that it leaves the impression that embracing the biblical promises about finances is being greedy. Fortunately, we can receive God's promises to prosper and enjoy good success without falling into the sinful trap of covetousness. One way is by meditating and delighting in Scripture. Meditation restrains greed, because biblical meditation puts observing and practicing the Word of God first above all other things. Meditation will allow us to have material things **and** keep our focus on the Lord (for more about covetousness, see chapter 15).

Meditation Connects Us to the Ministry of the Holy Spirit

The ministry of the Holy Spirit is to guide the Church into the truth. He was sent by God to live and abide in us and be our teacher and our guide. The Word of God is a foundational point of contact with the ministry of the Holy Spirit, because the Holy Spirit will not lead us out beyond the Word of God. Jesus said that the Holy Spirit would only speak what he hears and take what is Christ's and make it known to us (John 16:12–15). Because Jesus is the Word, the Holy Spirit will lead in line with the Word.

We can trust the Holy Spirit to lead us in this area of prosperity. If we are getting into the danger zone of greed and covetousness, he will be faithful to warn us. In addition, we can trust the Holy Spirit to give us godly desires. With godly desire comes faith and expectation. Spirit-led believers are able to discern the difference between the abundance that comes from God and that which does not.

Being led by the Spirit is a process, just as developing in any other Christian virtue is a process. It does no good to throw stones at young Christians trying to follow God and be led by the Holy Spirit. All Christians who accept this privilege will make mistakes at some point. However, as believers grow, they will recognize the leading of the Holy Spirit better, and the Holy Spirit will lead them into all truth.

An Example of Meditation

Let us walk through an example of biblical meditation. The Scripture says:

> [10] The name of the Lord is a strong tower; the righteous man runs into it and is safe.
>
> Proverbs 18:10 (ESV)

Although reading that Scripture once may not have much of an impact, meditation on that verse brings us to where we can say, *The name of the Lord is **my** strong tower, and **I** run to it and am safe. No matter what is happening in the circumstances of my life, I have safety and security in the name of the Lord.*

Do you see the difference? It is one thing to read Scripture and another thing to confess Scripture in a positive, affirming way. Meditating on Scripture is verbally confessing that Scripture, allowing it to infiltrate every area of your life. We begin to see God reaching toward us through the Scripture.

We might then confess that Scripture, and later in the day, hear a bad report, perhaps about the economy or a personal financial situation. As we develop in meditation and confession, our fears about bad news is replaced by our faith in spiritual truth. And our faith is not in vain. Faith in the truth of God's Word will lead to a change in the facts of our circumstances. Meditation and confession is the bridge that gets us there.

David was an absolute master of the art of meditation, and this discipline of meditation served him well in key moments of his life. Do you remember when David faced off against Goliath? His response to the taunts of Goliath is one of the greatest examples of a believer speaking forth the Word of God to manifest deliverance:

> [45] Then David said to the Philistine, "You come to me with a sword and with a spear and with a javelin, but I come to you in the name of the LORD of hosts, the God of the armies of Israel, whom you have defied.
>
> [46] This day the LORD will deliver you into my hand, and I will strike you down and cut off your head. And I will give the dead bodies of the host of the Philistines this day to the birds of the air and to the wild beasts of the earth, that all the earth may know that there is a God in Israel,
>
> [47] and that all this assembly may know that the LORD saves not with sword and spear. For the battle is the LORD's, and he will give you into our hand."
>
> I Samuel 17:45–47 (ESV)

There was not a single Scripture yet written that specifically said David would kill Goliath. How then could he have the audacity to say what the Lord was going to do for him that day? It is because, during all those years while he was herding sheep and serving his father, David had meditated on the covenant that God had made with Israel. He had delighted in the Word of God and knew what God said. Therefore, David realized that Goliath's defiance of Israel was defiance of God himself, and that David had the absolute right to not only resist Goliath, but also to expect that God would deliver Goliath into his hand **now**. To the other soldiers, their covenant was an abstract concept. Maybe God would help them, maybe he would not, but either way, they were not going to discover by facing Goliath. To David, it was a reality that could be trusted and acted on. What David said was exactly what he did. The action part underscores the purpose of meditation.

Failing to Meditate Means Failing to Prosper

Successfully acting on the Scriptures first requires meditating on the Scriptures. Could this be another reason that Christians fail to receive material blessings? It may not be the prosperity teaching that is faulty, but the fact that people are neglecting to do the principles necessary to manifest prosperity.

The consequences of neglect expose why the enemy would resist any teaching in the Church on money. As long as Satan can deceive us into thinking that money is evil and that poverty is piety, we will gloss over any scriptural teaching on money. We will not meditate on the truth of God about prosperity, and, therefore, we will not experience a manifestation of divine, financial blessing.

Train Yourself to Meditate

You do not have to close your eyes and sit cross-legged in a quiet place to meditate. You can meditate on the Scripture while driving to work, while doing chores, or during recess. You can train yourself to meditate at a moment's notice and in a variety of situations.

Meditation on the Word leads to prosperity. In the next chapter, we will see that the apostle John taught that divine prosperity includes money.

Divine Prosperity Includes Money

DIVINE PROSPERITY INCLUDES MORE than money, but it also includes money. Remember, money is only a part of God's provision, and, therefore, we should not become solely focused on money and neglect the other aspects of prosperity. However, it is important to give attention to the money part as well.

The apostle John's prayer in his letter to Gaius is significant because John establishes that the prosperity he believed in and prayed for included financial well-being. In his brief letter to Gaius, he gives us some details about Gaius' life that make his reference to finances unmistakable:

> [5] Beloved, it is a faithful thing you do in all your efforts for these brothers, strangers as they are,
>
> [6] who testified to your love before the church. You will do well to send them on their journey in a manner worthy of God.
>
> [7] For they have gone out for the sake of the name, accepting nothing from the Gentiles.
>
> [8] Therefore we ought to support people like these, that we may be fellow workers for the truth.
>
> 3 John 1:5–8 (ESV)

Gaius was committed to financing the Gospel, and was so diligent in his support of the ministry that he was known in the church for his giving. Gaius made sure visiting ministers were fed, clothed, and cared for properly. When they went out to evangelize in other places, he sent them on their way with monetary offerings and provisions to speed them along. John's prayer was that the Lord would prosper Gaius materially and financially so this act of service would continue.

John noted that the traveling preachers "took nothing from the Gentiles." Gentiles refer to non-believers, and John is teaching believers to take responsibility to fund the Gospel. Believers are justified in praying for financial well-being so they can support the ministry.

In his letter, the apostle John is revealing the twin purposes of divine financial prosperity: to meet the needs of the child of God, and to empower the child of God to be a financial blessing to others. Therefore, John's letter is a compelling argument that it is God's will for Christians to prosper financially.

Notably, John taught the Church that the believer's prosperity is directly tied to our *soul prosperity*. The believer prospers by meditating on the Word of God to obey carefully the Word of God. In the next section, we will see that in teaching about prosperity, the apostle John revealed a scriptural truth that reaches all the way back to the beginning.

PART 2
PROSPERITY IN THE BEGINNING

Man was Made to Prosper

THE BOOK OF GENESIS reveals God's original plan and intent for man and this planet. Genesis provides a perspective of man[9] and the earth that complements divine prosperity.

In the beginning, God created mankind not as an afterthought nor as an experiment, but as the crowning achievement of his creation. The order of the creation account is exceptionally deliberate in positioning human beings in an exalted status over all other created things. God created insects, birds, fish, and mammals and called them good, but man was created in God's **image and likeness.**

> [26] God said, Let Us [Father, Son, and Holy Spirit] make mankind in Our image, after Our likeness, and let them have complete authority over the fish of the sea, the birds of the air, the [tame] beasts, and over all of the earth, and over everything that creeps upon the earth.
>
> [27] **So God created man in His own image, in the image and likeness of God He created him;** male and female He created them.
>
> [28] And God blessed them and said to them, Be fruitful, multiply, and fill the earth, and subdue it [using all its vast resources in the service of God and man]; and have dominion over

the fish of the sea, the birds of the air, and over every living creature that moves upon the earth.

Genesis 1:26–28 (Amplified)

In His Image and Likeness

An image or a likeness is that which resembles something else. A photograph of you is the likeness of you. A sculpture of you is the likeness of you. God intentionally created Adam and Eve after his likeness so they would be like God. Therefore, we could easily say that God created man to be a success, to be prosperous and to be significant. Man was created to be this way, because God is not a failure and the man that God created in his image and likeness was not created to be a failure either.

A husband and wife who bring a child into this world have the glorious privilege of nurturing a life that is in their image and after their likeness. When that baby comes home from the hospital, the loved ones crowd around, saying, *She has her daddy's nose*, or *He has his mother's eyes*. The baby has the image of his or her parents. Clearly, the proud parents wish the best for their newborn. They would not hold up their newborn to heaven and say, *I pray my baby grows up to be a failure. I pray that he will be poor, sick, and defeated.* No! The prayer of rational parents is for the success of their child. This innate parental instinct comes from God. God is the first father, the preeminent parent. By definition, therefore, a God-created person is created to prosper.

Purpose and Prosperity

God created man to have a purpose. This purpose was to have complete authority over all the creatures on the earth and the very earth itself. Man's purpose figures as prominently as the creation of man, which indicates that creation and purpose go together.

Scientific theories of the origin of man usually leave out God's role and purpose in creating man. If humans were merely the chance result of eons of complex mutations, it would be easy to believe that their purpose, as well as their poverty or prosperity, was simply a matter of randomness. The fact that God **handcrafted** man shows that God, who is good, had goodness in store for man. Part of the goodness that God gave to man was man's purpose; therefore, God's purpose for man is a **prosperity purpose**. The creation account reinforces that there is no divine prosperity apart from divine purpose.

God showed Adam his purpose through his relationship with Adam. Adam walked and talked with God in the cool of the day. God was his father, his master, his teacher, his friend, and provider. Importantly, God revealed to his son Adam his purpose for being created:

> [28] And God blessed them. And God said to them, "Be fruitful and multiply and fill the earth and subdue it and have dominion over the fish of the sea and over the birds of the heavens and over every living thing that moves on the earth."
>
> Genesis 1:28 (ESV)

This passage of Scripture reveals that one aspect of God's purpose was for man to have complete authority over everything on the earth. God had set man up as a ruler of the entire planet in its unspoiled, pre-fallen state. This reveals God's boundless love and confidence in his man, and this divine grant of authority is difficult for mortal minds to comprehend. David sang about this wonder in the Psalms:

> ³ When I consider thy heavens, the work of thy fingers, the moon and the stars, which thou hast ordained;
>
> ⁴ What is man, that thou art mindful of him? and the son of man, that thou visitest him?
>
> ⁵ For thou hast made him a little lower than the angels, and hast crowned him with glory and honour.
>
> ⁶ **Thou madest him to have dominion over the works of thy hands; thou hast put all things under his feet**
>
> Psalms 8:3-6 (KJV)

David, under the inspiration of the Holy Spirit, calls man a ruler over the earth. Man was to rule the vast resources of the earth and to use these resources for the service of God **and man**. These resources included gold, silver, and other precious things. Genesis records that God made gold and silver and precious things, and called them good (Genesis 2:12). Moreover, gold and the other precious resources of the earth were created to be controlled by people. We could summarize man's status in the following ways:

- **God created Adam in his image and likeness.** God intended man to be like himself, which means that man was not created to be a failure or to be poor. The scriptural record of God creating man and endowing him with purpose disproves the notion that man was created by chance, evolving over millions of years in an indifferent universe absent of God's oversight.

- **Adam and Eve were sons of God.** The Genesis account makes it clear that Adam and Eve were the highest and best of all that God created. They enjoyed a special relationship with God like no other creature, including angels. The relationship that Adam and Eve had with God was a *love relationship*.

- **God made Adam and Eve lords of the earth.** God created Adam and Eve to reign and have dominion over the earth. The earth, and everything in it, was subject to Adam.

- **God created Adam and Eve to procreate.** God created Adam and Eve to produce offspring who would fill the whole earth and individually walk in the regal status and dominion of their parents. This mandate to multiply shows that God planned prosperity for the entire family of man.

- **Adam was the steward of the earth; therefore, his prosperity was bound to his stewardship.** God did not give ownership of creation to Adam. Instead, he gave the responsibility of creation to Adam. Adam's access to the prosperity of the earth depended on his obedience and service to God. When Adam rebelled, he lost his stewardship and his prosperity.

The Earth was Designed for Prosperity

God did not only create man to prosper, but he created the earth to prosper. In creating the earth, God created the ultimate bio-machine that could sustain and replenish itself and to be a source of unlimited and unending prosperity for the family of man **forever**. When God created the earth, he blessed this planet with the remarkable ability to bring forth life (Genesis 1:11–13), and ordained that the earth would replenish itself in part through the law of seedtime and harvest.

The simple seed was God's way of ensuring that necessary resources would be perpetuated to accommodate humanity throughout an eternity of generations. For example, consider the apple. One can easily count the seeds in an apple, but it is impossible for the human mind to comprehend the apples in a seed! Just one seed, when planted, produces a tree, which produces bushels of apples every season, year after year. Therefore, there are nearly an unlimited number of apples in each apple seed. This was especially true of the original creation, as no pests or diseases or other adverse conditions could ruin a harvest.

Modern man frets about how the earth is running out of resources: clean water, oil, natural gas, food supplies, and so on. However, God did not create the world to run out of anything. The earth is the greatest self-sustaining entity that humanity knows anything about, and it was designed to accommodate multiplied abundance.

When God spoke the plants and animals into existence, he blessed them with an ability to multiply. After God was through with creation, the seas were not empty. They were teeming with life. The continents were not barren; they were lush with the most beautiful vegetation and diverse animal life this planet has ever known. Every living thing was working to fulfill God's mandate to reproduce and multiply. In addition, every living thing on the earth was subject to Adam.

Most significantly, Adam and Eve were blessed and commanded to multiply. God fully intended man to fill the earth completely. All the descendants of Adam and Eve would be part of God's family. They would all rule and reign. In God's plan, there was no inferior class of people. In God's economy, every person was meant to have all the abundance they would ever need, enough to fulfill God's plan for their lives.

Man's Terrestrial Source of Prosperity

From a material perspective, everything Adam needed was already in the earth or the earth was already capable of producing it. If Adam were hungry, he did not have to ask God to give him food. The earth already had every kind of delicious food for him to eat. The earth also had every kind of raw material: timber, stone, oil, diamonds, gold, wind, and water for Adam to employ in fulfilling his directive to exercise dominion.

This truth is significant for the Church because the material resources the Church needs are already in the earth. They may be hidden, or temporarily in the hands of the ungodly, but they are in the earth. For this reason, it is important to adjust our thinking. In heaven, there are no factories, nor are there car dealerships, clothing stores, or banks. Every material thing we need is in the earth, or can be produced from the raw materials already in the earth.

In the next section, we will examine the impact of sin on man and creation, and of how that relates to the prosperity that God originally intended for the Church.

PART 3
PROSPERITY AND REDEMPTION

Man's Fall from Prosperity

THE SCRIPTURE SAYS IN Genesis:

> [8] And they heard the sound of the Lord God walking in the garden in the cool of the day, and the man and his wife hid themselves from the presence of the Lord God among the trees of the garden.
>
> [9] But the Lord God called to the man and said to him, "Where are you?"
>
> [10] And he said, "I heard the sound of you in the garden, and I was afraid, because I was naked, and I hid myself."
>
> [11] He said, "Who told you that you were naked? Have you eaten of the tree of which I commanded you not to eat?"
>
> [12] The man said, "The woman whom you gave to be with me, she gave me fruit of the tree, and I ate."
>
> [13] Then the Lord God said to the woman, "What is this that you have done?" The woman said, "The serpent deceived me, and I ate."
>
> Genesis 3:8–13 (ESV).

Tragically, Adam and Eve rebelled, and in doing so forfeited their divine honor and glory and came under the rule and influence of Satan. Instead of serving God, man began to express the sin nature that had lodged itself into his spirit. That is why after the Fall, man's life on the earth has been marked by evil, depravity, and violence.

The introduction of sin also brought about a radical corruption of the earth. The earth had been a place of inestimable abundance and prosperity, but after the Fall, the earth became cursed. It became a dangerous and unpredictable environment marked by natural disasters, blight, and pestilence. In the pre-fallen world, the lion lay down with the lamb. Now, a predator-prey relationship was established, as animals became wild and lethal.

Poverty began to appear in the fallen world. The earth no longer would yield its bounty to man, and man would have to eke out a living:

> ¹⁷ To Adam he said, "Because you listened to your wife and ate fruit from the tree about which I commanded you, 'You must not eat from it,' "Cursed is the ground because of you; through **painful toil** you will eat food from it all the days of your life.
> ¹⁸ It will produce thorns and thistles for you, and you will eat the plants of the field.
>
> Genesis 3:17–18 (NIV).

The phrase "painful toil" in the original language means *pain, labor, hardship, sorrow,* and *toil.* The same language is used in another part of Genesis:

> ²⁸ When Lamech had lived 182 years, he had a son.

Man's Fall from Prosperity

> ²⁹ He named him Noah and said, "He will comfort us in the labor and painful toil of our hands caused by the ground the LORD has cursed."
>
> Genesis 5:28-29 (NIV).

God created man to work but not to **toil**. Toil has the connotation of physically exhausting, backbreaking labor that is filled with regret.

God gave Adam work to do: to tend and keep the Garden, fill the earth, take dominion and rule over the earth, and employ the vast resources of the earth for the advancement of his kingdom. Adam worked to fulfill God's plan, but he did not work to survive because all his needs were already met in Eden.

After man's rebellion, man lost his connection to God and, because of this, the purpose of work became corrupted: man was now working to survive. Because the earth was no longer a cooperative source of prosperity, man now had to deal with lack. As men multiplied, they formed into tribes and nations and began to fight over resources. Tribes and nations pillaged one other and poverty and financial oppression became prevalent.

Words like *poor* and *poverty* have various nuances when used in Scripture. A person can be poor but not in poverty. For example, he might have only a few possessions compared with others, but be rich in spirit. If a poor person has faith in the promises of God, his present condition of financial lack is only **relative, circumstantial, and temporary**. Christ taught:

> [20] And he lifted up his eyes on his disciples, and said: "Blessed are you who are poor, for yours is the kingdom of God."
>
> Luke 6:20 (ESV).

In this passage, Jesus was talking to his **disciples.** Jesus was not saying that poor people are blessed because they are poor. He was saying that for those who follow God, though they may be poor in their circumstances, they are rich in God. For those who possess the kingdom of God are truly rich. Jesus was reminding them of that truth, which the apostle James echoes in his epistle:

> [5] Listen, my beloved brethren: Has not God chosen those who are poor in the eyes of the world to be rich in faith and in their position as believers and to inherit the kingdom, which He has promised to those who love Him?
>
> James 2:5 (Amplified).

Again, James is talking to and about believers. A believer may be poor materially in the eyes of this world, but in fact, they are rich in their inheritance in Christ. James is not saying that all poor people are rich in faith, or that to be rich in faith you have to be poor. Obviously, many poor people in the world do not have faith in the one true God. Instead, James is teaching the Church not to be a respecter of persons: just because a believer may be poor, it does not mean that their material lack reflects their spiritual condition.

Poverty, on the other hand, is primarily an effect of a spiritual condition. To be in poverty is the same as being separated from God and in complete bondage to sin. To be in poverty is to have no choices, no hope, and no faith that better days await. Are there people in the world completely severed from God? Absolutely! The apostle Paul wrote:

> ¹¹ Therefore remember that at one time you Gentiles in the flesh, called "the uncircumcision" by what is called the circumcision, which is made in the flesh by hands—
>
> **¹² remember that you were at that time separated from Christ, alienated from the commonwealth of Israel and strangers to the covenants of promise, having no hope and without God in the world.**
>
> Ephesians 2:11-12 (ESV).

Jesus said the poor are blessed because the kingdom of God belonged to them. However, he was talking to his disciples. Paul is describing a separate group here—not God's people. Paul describes them as *excluded from the citizenship in Israel*, and *without hope and without God in the world*. In other words, the unsaved have no legal access to the treasury of heaven. Because they have not received redemption, they are severed from the promises of God. Those in this state are in a far more dire and desperate condition than the poor who follow Jesus. This kind of poverty is enforced by the bondage that comes from sin. Moreover, even if the unbeliever prospers financially in this life, their prosperity is only temporary and passes away suddenly and permanently (Psalms 78:18–19).

Therefore, when I say that God did not create man to be in poverty, I am not condemning or denigrating poor people. People going through a difficult time financially have not necessarily fallen out of favor with the Lord, nor are they experiencing those problems because they do not have faith. What I am saying is that God created man to rule and to experience prosperity inwardly and outwardly. God did not create man to wear the shackles of spiritual, physical, and financial bondage and oppression. God created man to work, but he did not create him to toil. When God formed man out of the dust of the ground, he designed him, and **all** his descendants, to have lordship over this planet and to walk in dominion and abundance.

However, we also see from the creation account that the dominion and the material and financial prosperity accompanying God's blessing was conditional. Adam lost his dominion when he rebelled against God. Because Adam's material prosperity was tied to his relationship to God, he lost God's intended access to the unlimited bounty of the earth.

As poverty came because of sin, we should not regard poverty as a friend. Religion has elevated poverty to the status of piety, but poverty is against everything God designed in the beginning. God could have initially made the earth to be dull and barren; he did not. Instead, he created the earth to be lush and abundant. God could have made man to be a vagabond wandering the earth; he did not. Instead, he made his man to be a son and a ruler of the abundant resources of the earth. To reject this privilege and embrace poverty would be to disobey God's mandate.

The creation account in the book of Genesis lays an important foundation for the reality that God always wanted man to prosper.

However, when man fell from the original estate that God provided, was the promise of prosperity forever lost? No. After the Fall of man, God set a glorious plan of redemption in motion planned before the beginning of time and designed to restore man to glory. This magnificent plan of redemption included a restoration of the financial prosperity that Adam forfeited.

God's Recovery Plan

IN THE LAST CHAPTER, we examined how Adam's rebellion and sin had disastrous consequences for the estate of man and the earth in general. Although man fell from grace, his ruin was not permanent. God, in his perfect wisdom and grace, started his plan of redemption to recover his man.

What is Redemption?

Redemption means to buy back or pay a ransom to free from captivity. In a biblical context, God redeemed his people by paying in full their sin debt through the shed blood of Jesus of Nazareth. Put differently, man had a sin debt he could not pay, and Christ paid that debt through his death on the cross.

Redemption is not merely the payment of the sin debt, but also includes the sinner becoming an adopted heir of God. Through redemption, sinful man is brought back into fellowship with God and man's dominion and authority is recovered through his union with Christ Jesus.

The Three Clues of Redemption

After Adam and Eve sinned, God spoke about three signs, which pointed to his plan of redemption. These signs are articulated in the passages below:

> [14] So the LORD God said to the serpent:
>
> > "Because you have done this,
> > You are cursed more than all cattle,
> > And more than every beast of the field;
> > On your belly you shall go,
> > And you shall eat dust
> > All the days of your life.
>
> > [15] And I will put enmity
> > Between you and the woman,
> > **And between your seed** and her Seed;
> > He shall bruise your head,
> > And you shall bruise His heel."
>
> Genesis 3:14–15 (NKJV)

> [21] The LORD God made **garments of skin** for Adam and his wife and clothed them.
>
> Genesis 3:21 (NKJV)

> [23] therefore the LORD God sent him out of the garden of Eden to till the ground from which he was taken.
>
> [24] So He drove out the man, He placed cherubim at the east of the garden of Eden, and a flaming sword which turned every way, **to guard the way to the tree of life.**
>
> Genesis 3:23–24 (NKJV)

Let us examine the significance of these scenes from antiquity.

THE SEED OF THE WOMAN

The first clue that we have in Genesis 3 is the reference to the "seed" of the woman in verse 15. Many theologians believe this reference to the offspring of the woman is a reference to Jesus Christ, and in fact, the word "seed" is even capitalized in some popular English translations. The woman's "seed," or offspring, indicates that there will be a human bloodline that God will use to achieve his purposes of redemption. Indeed, a major theme of the Scripture is how God, from all the families on the earth, chose a particular lineage from which would appear the Messiah.

ANIMAL SKINS

Another clue of redemption is that after man sinned, God made garments of animal skin for Adam and Eve. Adam and Eve attempted to hide their nakedness by using fig leaves to cover themselves. However, God covered his man by slaying animals, skinning them, and preparing clothing from their hides. God was not only covering their nakedness, he was covering their sin! The Scripture says that without the shedding of blood, there is no forgiveness of sin (Hebrews 9:22). In slaying animals, God was indicating that the way back to Him would involve the blood sacrifice of a substitute.

The blood covenant (Genesis 15, Exodus 24:8, Luke 22:20) is central to God's plan of redemption. Jesus described his work as ushering in a new covenant based on the shedding of his blood:

> [19] And he took bread, and when he had given thanks, he broke it and gave it to them, saying, "This is my body, which is given for you. Do this in remembrance of me."
>
> [20] And likewise the cup after they had eaten, saying, "This cup that is poured out for you is the **new covenant in my blood**."
>
> Luke 22:19–20 (ESV)

When Jesus went to the cross, the shedding of his blood obliterated our sins, and is the basis of the Church's relationship with God (Hebrews 9).

THE TREE OF LIFE

The third clue refers to the tree of life. Genesis 2:9 records two trees of note: the tree of life and the tree of the knowledge of good and evil. God forbade man to eat of the tree of the knowledge of good and evil; however, no such prohibition was given for the tree of life (Genesis 2:16).

The tree of life represented man's life in God, and by eating its fruit, man would enjoy God's provision of unending fellowship. The tree of the knowledge of good and evil represented man's voluntary submission to God. By not eating of the tree, man would maintain the blessing of living in obedience to God. The tree of life, with the tree of the knowledge of good and evil, represented the relationship and submission necessary for man to walk in divine prosperity.

When Adam and Eve disobeyed God, they lost access to the Garden and to the tree of life specifically. In other words, they lost the eternal life that God had given them.

The Scripture says that God put in place cherubim (which the NET Bible translates as *angelic sentries*) and a flaming sword to guard the way to the tree of life. Although Adam was banished from the Garden, by protecting the way back to the tree of life, God was signaling that a time would come when man would again have access to the tree of life and eternal life. The book of Revelation confirms this:

> ⁷ He who has an ear, let him hear what the Spirit says to the churches. To the one who conquers I will grant to eat of the **tree of life**, which is in the paradise of God.
>
> Revelation 2:7 (ESV)

> ² through the middle of the street of the city; also, on either side of the river, the **tree of life** with its twelve kinds of fruit, yielding its fruit each month. The leaves of the tree were for the healing of the nations.
>
> ¹⁴ "Blessed are those who wash their robes, so that they may have the right to the **tree of life** and that they may enter the city by the gates."
>
> Revelation 22:2, 14 (ESV)

By preserving access to the tree of life, God demonstrates his intention to restore man through Jesus Christ.

The Redemptive Mystery

Taken together, the concepts of 1) the prophecy of a seed that would bruise the head of the serpent, 2) the introduction of the sacrifice of animals as a cover for man, and 3) God preserving a way to the tree of life for his man, are figurative languages that point to God's plan of redemption.

Genesis is a book filled with mystery and imagery that can be difficult to decode. For example, as important and fascinating as the creation story is, many details are not included. This allows many commentators and scholars to propose many theories about the serpent, the seed, and the tree of the knowledge of good and evil, and so forth. Even so, as believers, we can be confident of three important truths that apply here.

First is that the Scriptures teach that God planned for the redemption of man before the foundation of the world (Hebrews 4:3). This means that before there was an earth, before there was man, before there was anything created, God knew that he would create man, man would fall, and he would have a plan to rescue man from sin. Therefore, to think about God's statements and actions regarding a newly fallen Adam and Eve in the light of his redemptive plan is unconditionally consistent with Scripture.

Second, because Scripture progressively unfolds the plan of redemption, we can look back on the events of Genesis 1–3 and interpret them in the full light of the crucifixion, burial, and resurrection of Jesus Christ. God's reference to the "seed of the woman" could have meant many things; however, when considered in the light of the finished work of Christ, the reference becomes obvious.

Third, the Scriptures point us to Jesus and are ultimately about Jesus. Even the most obscure references in the Pentateuch can illustrate the life and work of Jesus Christ in profound ways. Discovering Christ in the creation account is indeed the natural aim of our study of these passages.

Although man fell from his glorious estate, God immediately began to reveal his perfect plan of redemption that would culminate in the advent of Jesus. An important key to redemption was God selecting a human bloodline, or seed, through which he would execute his plan. In the next chapter, we will explore God's selection of the focus of his chosen bloodline, Abraham's, and how God's dealings with Abraham reveal his will about divine prosperity.

Abraham's Inheritance

AS WE CONSIDER ABRAHAM, the concepts of the covenant and inheritance are foundational in our study of divine prosperity. Covenants were common in the days of Abraham. A covenant is a solemn agreement between two parties. For example, two tribes might make a blood covenant to defend and aid each other if attacked. In a blood covenant, the shedding of blood, usually the sacrifice of an animal, ratifies the agreement.

Blood covenants were not mere contractual arrangements, but were sacred agreements that represented the strongest type of pledge known to man. What made a covenant binding was the appeal to deity to watch over the covenant. Each party made a vow before their gods to keep the terms of the covenant, and understood that they would be cursed if they betrayed the agreement. Covenant breakers were despised and sometimes even killed for their treachery.

In the Bible, words like *oath*, *vow*, and *promise* are covenant words that have a dimension of meaning that often escapes modern readers. Today we make promises and vows all the time and break them without a thought. However, God's promises are covenant oaths that cannot be broken. The writer of Hebrews explains why God condescended to make a covenant with Abraham:

> [13] For when God made a promise to Abraham, since he had no one greater by whom to swear, he swore by himself,
>
> [14] saying, "Surely I will bless you and multiply you."
>
> [15] And thus Abraham, having patiently waited, obtained the promise.
>
> [16] For people swear by something greater than themselves, and in all their disputes an oath is final for confirmation.
>
> [17] So when God desired to show more convincingly to the heirs of the promise the unchangeable character of his purpose, he guaranteed it with an oath,
>
> [18] so that by two unchangeable things, in which it is impossible for God to lie, we who have fled for refuge might have strong encouragement to hold fast to the hope set before us.
>
> Hebrews 6:13–18 (ESV)

God sealed his promise to Abraham by entering into a blood covenant with him (Genesis 15), and he reiterated his covenant promise with an oath. Because God cannot lie, he did not need to take an oath that he would bless Abraham. However, God chose to do so to impress on Abraham the unchangeableness of his purpose (Genesis 22). Having God's promise **and** his oath, Abraham would have reason to believe that everything God had promised him would be fulfilled, though Abraham would not live to see all of God's promises to him manifested. By faith

Abraham saw these promises fulfilled, especially the promise of the coming Savior (John 8:56).

The concept of covenant is significant to the believer because our relationship with God is in fact a covenant. The New Testament could also be called the New Covenant, and it is a covenant secured by the shed blood of Christ (Luke 22:20).

The word, *inheritance* is also a covenant word. Again, modern people usually understand inheritance as an estate that is received because of a loved one's passing, as in children inheriting property from their parents. However, in the Bible, *inheritance* means *a possession*, not necessarily obtained because of the passing of a relative. To quote *Vines Expository Dictionary of New Testament Words*, the meaning of inheritance "broadens out to include all spiritual good provided through and in Christ, and particularly all that is contained in the hope grounded on the promises of God."[10] In short, when a person is in covenant **with** God, he will receive an inheritance **from** God.

The concept of covenant inheritance, or God-given possession, runs throughout Scripture. For example, the nation of Israel was founded on the inheritance that God had promised to Abraham (first called Abram):

> [1] When Abram was ninety-nine years old the LORD appeared to Abram and said to him, "I am God Almighty; walk before me, and be blameless,
>
> [2] that I may make my covenant between me and you, and may multiply you greatly."

> ⁷ And I will establish my covenant between me and you and your offspring after you throughout their generations for an everlasting covenant, to be God to you and to your offspring after you.
>
> ⁸ And I will give to you and to your offspring after you the land of your sojournings, all the land of Canaan, **for an everlasting possession**, and I will be their God."
>
> Genesis 17:1–2, 7–8 (ESV)

> ⁸ By faith Abraham obeyed when he was called to go out to a place that he was to **receive as an inheritance**. And he went out, not knowing where he was going.
>
> Hebrews 11:8 (ESV)

These Scriptures show the relationship between covenant and inheritance; by entering into covenant with God, Abraham received an inheritance,[11] the land of Canaan. In fact, Abraham's inheritance included everything that God promised to Abraham. In his book, *What Are Abraham's Blessings Anyway?*, Dr. Jay Snell identifies at least sixty promises that God made to Abraham as recorded in Genesis.[12] This included Abraham being given a noble name, having many descendants, having descendants who would be kings, protection from his enemies, and immense wealth, including silver, gold, livestock, and servants. God received an inheritance as well. Through Abraham, he secured a lineage through whom the Redeemer would come, and received a people he could call his own. Indeed, God considers his people–the seed of Abraham which includes the Church–as his inheritance (Deuteronomy 7:6, Ephesians 1:18).

As we will explore more fully in later sections, God has given the Church an inheritance through Christ. All the blessings and promises of the New Covenant, including prosperity, are covenant possessions given to us by a holy God who cannot lie and will not arbitrarily change his mind. When God says he wants us to be blessed, prosperous, and healed, he is not playing games. It is not a fantasy, but a settled promise sealed with an unbreakable oath.

Abraham's Inheritance is Spiritual

Although Abraham's inheritance included material blessings, the most significant aspect of his inheritance was a spiritual blessing. God said, "All peoples of the earth will be blessed through you." (Genesis 12:3, 22:18). The apostle Paul explains what the blessing God gave to Abraham was:

> ⁶ just as Abraham "BELIEVED GOD, AND **IT WAS ACCOUNTED TO HIM FOR RIGHTEOUSNESS.**"
>
> Galatians 3:6 (NKJV)

The blessing that came to Abraham was to be declared righteous by God. Righteousness is purely being right with God. When God made Abraham righteous, he forgave Abraham's sins, called Abraham his friend and positioned Abraham to receive all of his blessings, including spiritual, physical, and financial blessings. God did this not because of Abraham's good works, but because Abraham believed God.

The Material Aspects of Abraham's Inheritance

Although Abraham's blessing is spiritual, it **includes** material provision. The Lord blessed Abraham with righteousness **and** with abundant financial wealth, because finances were part of the covenant inheritance. We know this because the Scriptures teach that **God** made Abraham rich. Abraham's wealth had a spiritual dimension to it, because God was causing his wealth to multiply.

Certainly, Abraham's extraordinary wealth was inferior to the greater blessing of righteousness, but not contradictory to it. These blessings were complementary because they came from the same source. As the Scripture says:

> [2] **Now Abram was extremely rich in livestock and in silver and in gold.**
>
> Genesis 13:2 (Amplified)

> [1] Abraham was now very old, and the **LORD had blessed him in every way.**
>
> Genesis 24:1 (NIV)

> [1] Abraham was now a very old man. **The LORD had made him rich, and he was successful in everything he did.**
>
> Genesis 24:1 (CEV)

> [34] So he said, "I am Abraham's servant.
>
> [35] **The LORD has greatly blessed my master, and he has become great.** He has given him flocks and herds, silver and gold, male servants and female servants, camels and donkeys.

Abraham's Inheritance

> ³⁶ And Sarah my master's wife bore a son to my master when she was old, and to him he has given all that he has.
>
> Genesis 24:34-36 (CEV)

To be blessed like Abraham is to be blessed in every way: spiritually, mentally, and physically (that includes health and longevity), materially, and financially. This is in harmony with a Scripture that we referenced earlier:

> ² Beloved, I pray that you may prosper in all things and be in health, just as your soul prospers.
>
> 3 John 1:2 (NKJV)

The Scripture presents the father of our faith, without contradiction, as a man who was spiritually righteous and extremely rich financially. Both the righteousness and the material wealth came from God, and both were part of Abraham's inheritance.

Abraham's Inheritance is for His Descendants

This covenant inheritance was not only given to Abraham, but also passed on to his descendants. Just as God made Abraham wealthy, God also worked in Isaac's life to make him wealthy too:

> ¹¹ After the death of Abraham, **God blessed Isaac** his son. And Isaac settled at Beer-lahai-roi.
>
> Genesis 25:11 (ESV)

> ² And the LORD appeared to him and said, "Do not go down to Egypt; dwell in the land of which I shall tell you.

> ³ Sojourn in this land, and I will be with you and will bless you, **for to you and to your offspring I will give all these lands, and I will establish the oath that I swore to Abraham your father.**
> ⁴ I will multiply your offspring as the stars of heaven and will give to your offspring all these lands. And in your offspring all the nations of the earth shall be blessed,
> ⁵ because Abraham obeyed my voice and kept my charge, my commandments, my statutes, and my laws."
>
> Genesis 26:2–5 (ESV)

God confirms Isaac in Abraham's covenant and gives Isaac the blessing of Abraham including wealth:

> ¹² And Isaac sowed in that land and reaped in the same year a hundredfold. The LORD blessed him,
> ¹³ and the man became rich, and gained more and more until he became very wealthy.
> ¹⁴ He had possessions of flocks and herds and many servants, so that the Philistines envied him.
>
> Genesis 26:12–14 (ESV)

The verdict is unmistakable. The covenant wealth of Abraham was passed to Isaac. Isaac not only inherited everything that belonged to Abraham (Genesis 25:5) but also was himself supernaturally blessed by God, such that he reaped one hundredfold within a twelve-month period.

If Isaac's financial state were of no consequence to believers today, then there would be no point in the Scripture providing such detail and emphasis on his wealth. The Holy Spirit is making the point that the blessing of Abraham was multifaceted and that wealth was an important part of it. The blessing of Abraham was intended to be passed down to Abraham's descendants and wealth was included in that bestowal.

Abraham's grandson, Jacob, had a difficult life, but he also experienced supernatural prosperity when God transferred the wealth of his uncle, Laban, to him:

> [43] In this way the man grew exceedingly prosperous and came to own large flocks, and female and male servants, and camels and donkeys.
>
> Genesis 30:43 (ESV; refer also to verses 25-33)

I so appreciate the superlatives of Scripture. Abraham was not just rich; he was **extremely rich** in silver, gold, and livestock. Isaac was not just successful; Isaac reaped one hundredfold in a single year and became **extremely wealthy**. Jacob did not have only his needs barely met; he grew **exceedingly prosperous** and came to own large flocks. This is the language of prosperity, and Isaac and Jacob enjoyed the same material prosperity that Abraham enjoyed because they were heirs with Abraham of the same promise:

> [9] By faith he went to live in the land of promise, as in a foreign land, living in tents with Isaac and Jacob, **heirs with him of the same promise.**
>
> Hebrews 11:9 (ESV)

That is the point. Abraham, Isaac, and Jacob were not wealthy because they were shrewd business people. It was not because they had a genetic talent to make money. They were blessed! God made them rich. Against all odds, when they might have starved amid famine, when ruthless pagan kings might have killed them, when conspiring relatives were seeking to cheat them, God turned the tables and caused abundant money to come into their hands! This is why we say that the wealth of Abraham was a spiritual blessing with material effect. God was working out his plan in the financial area of their lives as well.

Abraham's Inheritance is for National Israel

It is tempting to think that God's blessings on Abraham, Isaac, and Jacob were for them alone. However, God told Abraham that he would not only bless Abraham but **all** of Abraham's descendants:

> ⁶ I will make you exceedingly fruitful, and I will make you into nations, and kings shall come from you.
>
> ⁷ And I will establish my covenant between **me and you and your offspring after you throughout their generations** for an everlasting covenant, to be God to you and to your offspring after you.
>
> Genesis 17:6–7 (ESV)

God included the nation of Israel in the Abrahamic covenant at Mount Sinai, and in doing so, God passed the blessing of Abraham to the nation, as recorded in Deuteronomy 28:

> ¹ "And if you faithfully obey the voice of the LORD your God, being careful to do all his commandments that I command

Abraham's Inheritance

you today, the LORD your God will set you high above all the nations of the earth.

² **And all these blessings shall come upon you and overtake you**, if you obey the voice of the LORD your God.

³ Blessed shall you be in the city, and blessed shall you be in the field.

⁴ Blessed shall be the fruit of your womb and the fruit of your ground and the fruit of your cattle, the increase of your herds and the young of your flock.

⁵ Blessed shall be your basket and your kneading bowl.

⁶ Blessed shall you be when you come in, and blessed shall you be when you go out.

¹¹ **And the LORD will make you abound in prosperity**, in the fruit of your womb and in the fruit of your livestock and in the fruit of your ground, within the land that the LORD swore to your fathers to give you.

Deuteronomy 28:1-6, 11 (ESV)

God's promises to the nation of Israel closely match the blessings that he gave to Abraham. It was God's intent to make the **entire nation** wealthy and prosperous. Because God is all-powerful, all things are possible with Him; it makes no difference whether he is making one person rich or a nation of millions.

Therefore, at Mount Sinai, God extended to Israel the same measure and quality of blessing that he gave to their ancestor, Abraham. For Israel to receive these blessings would be equivalent to them receiving the inheritance that God had provided to them. Moses spoke the blessings of the covenant over Israel, and the language of wealth, blessing, and abundance in these Scriptures is strong, clear, and unmistakable.

The Blessing and the Law

The blessings God spoke to Moses were part of what came to be known as the Mosaic Law (or "the Law"). The Law represented the precepts and judgments of God, explaining right from wrong and instructing Israel how to live. The Law detailed the abundant blessings Israel would enjoy if they obeyed God, and recited the astonishing curses that would come upon people if they forsook God.

Why did God give the Law at this point? One reason is that in giving Israel the Law, God gave his chosen people the privilege to be custodians of his Word. No other nation in history has been so honored.

Second, in giving the Law, God provided Israel instruction on how to live and how they were different from the surrounding nations. Israel's obedience to the Law would make them a light and witness to the Gentile nations (Deuteronomy 4:6–8).

Third, the Law revealed God's holiness and man's depravity. The righteous standard of the Law and the sacrificial system designed to cover sins impressed on the Israelites their sin and the need for a final sacrifice: One who would come and take away the sins of people for the last time. Therefore, the Law and the Prophets testified to Israel of the righteousness of God in Christ Jesus.

Further, because the Law revealed God's standard of righteousness, it effectively condemned all men—whether Jew or Gentile—because all men sin.

In Galatians 3, the apostle Paul described the Law as an "addendum" to the Abrahamic covenant and as a "tutor" that guided and prepared the Jews for the coming of Christ. Paul argued that the Law did not replace or undermine the Abrahamic covenant and its promises, especially the promise to receive righteousness by faith. God imposed on Israel the Law—with its moral code, ceremonial obligations, and priestly sacrifices—to restrain their sin and finally guide them to faith in Christ.

In short, the Law did not replace the Abrahamic covenant, but introduced an added requirement for the nation of Israel. When Christ came and finished his work of salvation, this added requirement was fulfilled, but the Abrahamic covenant and its blessing—receiving righteousness by faith—remained. However, because the prosperity promises of the Law are so explicit, Christians began to associate biblical prosperity with obedience to the Law rather than with the righteousness that comes by faith. Even some modern Christians, who deny the idea of prosperity for the Church, agree that God intended Israel to be financially blessed. However, we have seen that the financial blessings of God were not the exclusive province of the Law, but part of Abrahamic covenant that preceded the Law. Therefore, since the blessing of Abraham (that is, righteousness), belongs to the Church, then the financial part of the blessing belongs to the Church as well.

Abraham's Inheritance is for the Church

It is through Christ Jesus that the Church receives the blessing of Abraham:

> [6] just as Abraham "BELIEVED GOD, AND **IT WAS ACCOUNTED TO HIM FOR RIGHTEOUSNESS.**"
> [7] Therefore know that only those who are of faith are sons of Abraham.
> [8] And the Scripture, foreseeing that God would justify the Gentiles by faith, preached the gospel to Abraham beforehand, saying, "In you all the nations shall be blessed."
> [9] So then those who are of faith are blessed with believing Abraham.
> [16] Now to Abraham and his Seed were the promises made. He does not say, "**And to seeds**," as of many, but as of one, "And to your Seed," who is Christ.
>
> Galatians 3:6–9, 16 (NKJV)

Paul taught that Jesus Christ is the seed of Abraham, and points out that the promise is made to Abraham and his "Seed" who is Jesus. Although the Jews, indeed, are the physical descendants of Abraham; however, for inheriting the promises, the seed of Abraham is Jesus of Nazareth. Jesus is the means by which the Abrahamic blessing flows to the "sons of Abraham" which include Gentiles who trust Christ. The blessing of Abraham is righteousness (Romans 4 and Galatians 3) and, anyone who places his or her faith in Christ has become an inheritor of this blessing through their union with Christ.

As we examined earlier in this chapter, the Apostles taught although Israel had been required to keep the Law, the blessing of Abraham is received by faith, not by adhering to the Law. The Law levied on national Israel a conditional relationship to the blessing of Abraham. When they followed the Law to earn their righteousness, they inevitably fell short of the Law's requirements; therefore, they had to perform elaborate rituals and sacrifices to restore fellowship with God. However, Paul explains that the finished work of Christ, rather than the works of the Law, secures the believer's access to the blessing of Abraham, whether that believer is a Jew or Gentile. Jesus has perfectly fulfilled the obligations of the Law so in Christ, all the righteous requirements of the Law are met and all penalties against the believer for breaking God's law are duly satisfied. Therefore, for those who have faith in Christ, there are no legal deterrents from them receiving the blessing of Abraham:

> [38] "Therefore, my friends, I want you to know that through Jesus the forgiveness of sins is proclaimed to you.
>
> [39] Through him everyone who believes is set free from every sin, a justification you were not able to obtain under the law of Moses.
>
> Acts 13: 38–39 (NIV)

> [13] But Christ has rescued us from the curse pronounced by the law. When he was hung on the cross, he took upon himself the curse for our wrongdoing. For it is written in the Scriptures, "Cursed is everyone who is hung on a tree."

> ¹⁴ **Through Christ Jesus, God has blessed the Gentiles with the same blessing he promised to Abraham**, so that we who are believers might receive the promised Holy Spirit through faith.
>
> Galatians 3:13–14 (NLT)

> ⁴ For Christ has already accomplished the purpose for which the law was given. As a result, all who believe in him are made right with God.
>
> Romans 10:4 (NLT)

These Scriptures irrefutably connect the blessing of Abraham to the Church through Jesus Christ. Christ Himself is the mediator of this New Covenant; as the present-day High Priest, Christ ensures that all believers may receive the promised eternal inheritance (Hebrews 9:15).

Unfortunately, the Church has been bamboozled into thinking that the Abrahamic inheritance we received from God differs from what Abraham received. We have been taught that our inheritance in Christ is **spiritual and non-material** and that the financial component that Abraham enjoyed was **deleted.** Instead of walking in the financial blessing of Abraham, the Church has been mistakenly taught that God wants us to be poor. However, the Apostles taught that the blessing that Abraham received is the same blessing that the Church has received in Christ. This is why the promises of the New Testament cover both spiritual and natural needs.

In review, Abraham's inheritance included financial wealth. God prospered Abraham in every way imaginable, and these blessings were passed to Isaac, then Jacob, then to all of Abraham's descendants. The glory of the Gospel is that the believer, through faith in Christ, has become the seed of Abraham. Abraham is our spiritual father, and we have the same spiritual and material blessings that Abraham enjoyed.

In the next chapter, we will further examine our inheritance from the perspective of the writings in the New Testament.

PART 4
THE PROSPERITY OF OUR INHERITANCE IN CHRIST

Forgiveness of Sins

IN THE LAST SECTION, we learned that when God entered into covenant with Abraham, God gave Abraham the inheritance of righteousness, also known as the blessing of Abraham. God gave that inheritance not only to Abraham but also to Abraham's descendants. This includes the Church, because through Christ, the Church has become the seed of Abraham. Therefore, like Abraham, the Church has received an inheritance:

> [12] giving thanks to the Father **who has qualified us to be partakers of the inheritance of the saints in the light.**
>
> Colossians 1:12 (NKJV)

> [3] Blessed be the God and Father of our Lord Jesus Christ! According to his great mercy, he has caused us to be born again to a living hope through the resurrection of Jesus Christ from the dead,
>
> [4] **to an inheritance** that is imperishable, undefiled, and unfading, kept in heaven for you
>
> 1 Peter 1:3–4 (ESV)

Salvation is not just going to heaven after death, but includes a biblical inheritance that encompasses everything we have in

Christ. Phrases such as, *in Him, in whom, in Christ, by Christ* are common in the New Testament, and refer to those things which are part of the believer's inheritance. For example, the following is a classic *in Him* Scripture:

> ⁷ **In Him** we have redemption (deliverance and salvation) through His blood, the remission (forgiveness) of our offenses (shortcomings and trespasses), in accordance with the riches and the generosity of His gracious favor
>
> Ephesians 1:7 (Amplified)

We have redemption *in Him* or in Christ Jesus. This redemption is our inheritance in Christ and includes deliverance, salvation, and forgiveness of sins. The following is an *in Whom* Scripture, also by the apostle Paul:

> ¹² Giving thanks to the Father, Who has qualified and made us fit to share the portion which is the **inheritance of the saints** (God's holy people) in the Light.
>
> ¹³ [The Father] has delivered and drawn us to Himself out of **the control and the dominion of darkness** and has transferred us into the kingdom of the Son of His love,
>
> ¹⁴ **In Whom** we have our redemption through His blood, [which means] the forgiveness of our sins.
>
> Colossians 1:12-14 (Amplified)

Paul is teaching that the believer's inheritance in Christ includes the forgiveness of sins and deliverance from the dominion of Satan.

Bound by Sin

When Adam and Eve sinned, they plunged the entire human race into sin, and all their descendants were born in sin. This sin nature not only aligned us with Satan, but also carried the penalty of death with it. When Ezekiel stated, "the soul who sins shall die" (Ezekiel 18:4), he was articulating a spiritual law (Romans 5).

Death has more than one meaning in Scripture. For example, although death may mean to cease to live physically, it may also mean spiritual separation from God. For example, in the Garden of Eden, God gave Adam this solemn warning:

> [16] But the LORD told him, "You may eat fruit from any tree in the garden,
>
> [17] except the one that has the power to let you know the difference between right and wrong. If you eat any fruit from that tree, you will die before the day is over!"
>
> Genesis 2:16–17 (CEV)

When Adam and Eve ate from that tree, they died **spiritually** that day, but their physical death came much later. The effect of spiritual death on the human race was the introduction and escalation of iniquity; such that God was prepared to wipe out all of mankind (Genesis 6:5–8). However, it was not until the Mosaic Law was given that mankind had an explicit explanation of sin and its impact.

As stated in chapter 8, the Law was the body of commandments that God gave to Moses and explained right and wrong and the consequences of either path. The Law articulated God's standard of holiness and perfection, and highlighted man's utter inability to meet that standard on his own.

Although a person might be successful in keeping parts of the Law, no one could keep all of it. The apostle James explains that to break the Law in just one point is to be guilty of breaking all of it (James 2:10–11). Jesus taught that keeping the Law was not merely about actions, but also involved the motives and intents of people's hearts (as when he taught on adultery; Matthew 5:27–28).

Because sinful man could not possibly keep the Law, God set up a sacrificial system that would allow his people to receive forgiveness for their sins. This typically involved the Israelite priesthood ritualistically slaying animals to cover the sin of the transgressors. However, even with the sacrificial system in place, the blood of animals could not cover certain sins. For example, if a person cursed his parents or committed murder, the penalty for those acts was death. There was no sacrificial remedy for those sins. Therefore, all Israel stood condemned before God: if to break the Law in one point was to break the Law completely, then all Israel technically deserved to die. Additionally, the Law also spelled doom for non-Jews (Gentiles) as well. Although Gentiles were not explicitly given the Law, God has given all men conscience, that is, an innate sense of right and wrong. The unrighteous behavior of Gentiles showed that man, even with a minimum sense of righteousness hardwired into his soul, could not live up to the basic standards of righteousness. Therefore, all Gentiles stood convicted and without excuse before God. Indeed, as the apostle Paul wrote in Romans, "Jews and Gentiles alike are all under sin" that "every mouth may be silenced and the whole world held accountable to God" (Romans 3:9, 19).

The Curse of the Law

Justice demands that broken laws be punished. The guilt of all men before God for breaking his laws meant that all men deserved punishment, which included ruin, destruction, and finally death (physical and spiritual). Another word that the Scriptures use for these penalties is *curses*. The Law explained in detail what these curses were, and Paul referred to them collectively as the **curse of the Law** (Galatians 3:13).

The curse of the Law was neither random nor haphazard. It was an intentional, supernatural punishment for transgression. This is why, when God spoke the words of the Law to Israel, the sheer weight of its holiness and the doom associated with its transgression filled Israel with fear (Exodus 19:16–18). Although the curse of the Law is described throughout the Old Testament, it, with the blessings of the Law, is neatly summarized in Deuteronomy 28. The following is an example of some curses for disobeying the Law of God (read the entire chapter for full detail):

> [15] "But if you will not obey the voice of the LORD your God or be careful to do all his commandments and his statutes that I command you today, then all these curses shall come upon you and overtake you.

> [16] Cursed shall you be in the city, and cursed shall you be in the field.
>
> [17] Cursed shall be your basket and your kneading bowl.
>
> [18] Cursed shall be the fruit of your womb and the fruit of your ground, the increase of your herds and the young of your flock.
>
> [19] Cursed shall you be when you come in, and cursed shall you be when you go out.
>
> [20] "The LORD will send on you curses, confusion, and frustration in all that you undertake to do, until you are destroyed and perish quickly on account of the evil of your deeds, because you have forsaken me.
>
> [21] The LORD will make the pestilence stick to you until he has consumed you off the land that you are entering to take possession of it.
>
> Deuteronomy 28:15–21 (ESV)

Whereas God's blessing is his supernatural empowerment to succeed, the curse of the Law was his supernatural empowerment to fail. According to Deuteronomy, the curse of the Law could be summarized as poverty, sickness, and physical and spiritual death.[13]

There should be no doubt in our minds that the curse of the Law is **negative.** If God explicitly states that having an incurable disease is a curse, then we should see having an incurable disease as a negative condition, not a positive condition. If God says that crop failure, job loss, and persistent lack and hunger are part of the curse of the Law, then we need not argue that these calamities are blessings. Remember, **God** gave the Law to Moses. What he says is a blessing (namely, abundance, good health, and long life) and what he says is a curse (namely, persistent lack, terrible sicknesses, and premature death) is his perfect, holy revealed truth.

God's revelation of truth often contradicts man's ideas about truth. Although some religious doctrines teach that poverty and sickness are virtues, this notion does not align with Scripture.

The Curse of the Law is a Judgment from God

One may ask, *If God is good, then why would he punish people in such terrible ways?* The answer is that God is good **and** he is just. Although the penalties described in Scripture are severe, God's judgments are always consistent with his divine nature. The Scripture states that God works all things according to the good counsel of his will (Ephesians 1:11). Therefore, God's judgments are true, righteous, good, wise, and loving.

In certain Christian circles that embrace prosperity, there is a point of view that God does not bring negative judgment in the form of sickness, poverty, or adversity precisely because he is good. Therefore, God does not intentionally curse people, so their argument goes, but instead **he allows** curses to come upon people.

This view is debatable for many reasons of which we cannot explore in detail, but it is sufficient to say that there is no contradiction whatsoever between a God who actively judges and punishes sin and a God who blesses with prosperity for at least four reasons. First, both the curses and the blessings of the Law are a part of the Law, and, therefore, from God. Logic would not permit us to argue that the blessing of the Law comes from God, but the curse of the Law does not.

Second, the curse of the Law is about justice. God is a just judge, and there cannot be justice if there is no punishment. When a killer is tried and convicted of a heinous crime, the judge does not **allow** the offender to be sentenced; instead, he **renders** the verdict. When a police officer pulls over a motorist for speeding, he does not **allow** the motorist to get a ticket, he **issues** the ticket. In the same way, Deuteronomy 28 is a record of a just and holy God taking full responsibility for his active and intentional judgment of willful rebellion. Although the concept of God's wrath makes our 21st century sensibilities tingle, God's justice is as much a part of his nature as his goodness. We ought not to sacrifice one attribute to promote the other.

Third, if God only passively allows bad things happen to people then whole sections of Scripture become incomprehensible. Do we think God allowed the flood to come in Noah's day, or that he brought the flood? Did God sit by helplessly as the vials of judgment in the book of Revelation were opened, or did he authorize the terrible judgments that were poured out?

Finally, if God's wrath were somehow removed from the crucifixion, then the Church could not claim redemption. It was on the cross that Christ suffered God's judgment in our place. Isaiah wrote:

> [10] Yet it was the will of the LORD to crush him;
> He has put him to grief;
>
> Isaiah 53:10 (ESV)

The margin notes of the English Standard Version translate "he has put him to grief" as "he has made him sick." Christ bore our sin and sickness and if through Christ's suffering and sacrifice we fail to grasp the sinfulness of sin, and God's utter position against it, then we will not adequately understand the depth of God's grace in securing our redemption! The curse of the Law is a response to the radical corruption and the unspeakable sin of man. By establishing a penalty for sin, **God is taking a position against sin.** By providing a way of escape from judgment through Jesus Christ, **God is taking a position in favor of the believer.** That God punishes sin does not diminish the believer's ability to receive from the hand of a loving and good God.

Redeemed from Sin by Jesus Christ

Because the curse of the Law is from God, and in fact, is administered by God, then the redemptive act of Christ's work on the cross becomes all the more glorious. The words, "Christ redeemed us from the curse of the law by becoming a curse for us" (Galatians 3:13) become among the sweetest ever written. How was it that Christ became a curse for us?

Jesus was the only one who could save us all because, as God in the flesh, he could represent all men, and as a man who led a perfect life, he had satisfied the requirements of the Law and could stand before God as righteous. On the one side, there is the sinless Jesus, the God man who can represent the entire human race. On the other side is the fallen humanity. In redemption, God exchanged our sin for Christ's righteousness. Jesus became our substitute at the cross, bearing our sins, and then enduring the full punishment for those sins. God smote Jesus with the full fury of the curse of the Law and every penalty was meted out to the uttermost. Not one transgression or sin committed by man was left unpunished on the cross of Christ. That is why the apostle Paul writes that because of the cross:

> [14] God wiped out the charges that were against us for disobeying the Law of Moses. He took them away and nailed them to the cross.
>
> Colossians 2:14 (CEV)

Paul leaves no doubt that Christ's suffering released us from the curse of the Law and the wrath of God:

> [13] Christ redeemed us from the curse of the law **by becoming a curse for us**—for it is written, "Cursed is everyone who is hanged on a tree"—
>
> Galatians 3:13 (ESV)

> [8] but God shows his love for us in that while we were still sinners, Christ died for us.
> [9] Since, therefore, we have now been justified by his blood, much more shall we be saved by him **from the wrath of God**.
>
> Romans 5:8–9 (ESV)

We, as sinners, are saved from God's wrath because Christ took our place on the cross, and, therefore, we have been released from the entire curse of the Law. Any penalty or curse that should have come upon us was fully paid by Christ. For example, the Law lists sickness as a curse:

> [21] The LORD will plague you with diseases until he has destroyed you from the land you are entering to possess.
>
> [22] The LORD will strike you with wasting disease, with fever and inflammation, with scorching heat and drought, with blight and mildew, which will plague you until you perish.
>
> [61] The LORD will also bring on you every kind of sickness and disaster not recorded in this Book of the Law, until you are destroyed.
>
> Deuteronomy 28:21-22, 61 (NIV)

The believer is completely delivered from the curse of sickness listed in Deuteronomy. This deliverance is reiterated in the New Covenant:

> [24] He himself bore our sins in his body on the tree, that we might die to sin and live to righteousness. By his wounds you have been healed.
>
> 1 Peter 2:24 (ESV)

Note the utter financial failure and calamity under the curse of the Law:

> [18] Cursed shall be the fruit of your womb and the fruit of your ground, the increase of your herds and the young of your flock.
>
> [38] You shall carry much seed into the field and shall gather in little, for the locust shall consume it.
>
> Deuteronomy 28:18, 38 (ESV)

Note the provision of financial prosperity through Christ Jesus:

> ⁹ For you know the grace of our Lord Jesus Christ, that though he was rich, yet for your sake he became poor, so that you by his poverty might become rich.
>
> 2 Corinthians 8:9 (ESV)

Note the spiritual failure and death that the curse brings:

> ⁶⁴ "And the LORD will scatter you among all peoples, from one end of the earth to the other, and there you shall serve other gods of wood and stone, which neither you nor your fathers have known.
>
> ⁶⁵ And among these nations you shall find no respite, and there shall be no resting place for the sole of your foot, but the LORD will give you there a trembling heart and failing eyes and a languishing soul.
>
> Deuteronomy 28:64–65 (ESV)

However, Christ redeems us from spiritual death:

> ⁴ But God, being rich in mercy, because of the great love with which he loved us,
>
> ⁵ even when we were dead in our trespasses, made us alive together with Christ—by grace you have been saved—
>
> ⁶ and raised us up with him and seated us with him in the heavenly places in Christ Jesus,
>
> ⁷ so that in the coming ages he might show the immeasurable riches of his grace in kindness toward us in Christ Jesus.
>
> Ephesians 2:4–7 (ESV)

The reality is that God took the legal bounty that was on our heads as lawbreakers, nailed it to the cross, and stamped on it *paid in full* and *justice has been fully executed.* Through the effective, finished work of Jesus Christ, the issue of the curse of the Law is forever settled for the believer. **It no longer applies to us!**

Set Free from Sin but Not Exempt from Suffering

It is fair and reasonable to introduce some clarifications at this point. Being set free from the curse of the Law is a legal reality that the believers must learn how to experience or manifest in their lives on the earth. For example, being adopted into the family of God means that all believers can now pray to the Father in Jesus' name. This is a legal reality. However, if the believer does not pray, then he will not experience the legal reality of prayer. Put another way, he will not experience the benefit of prayer that the Father has provided.

Similarly, although the Church is legally redeemed from the curse of the Law, it is our responsibility to manifest this legal reality in our daily lives. The fact of redemption does not exempt Christians from problems. We still have to obtain the promises of redemption through faith and patience. Indeed, it is the ministry of the Holy Spirit to teach us and guide us to live above sin, and above poverty, sickness, and all the other aspects of the curse of the Law. As we learn to yield to his guidance and place faith in his power, we will begin to manifest the spiritual realities of redemption in our lives despite contrary circumstances (for more on the relationship between suffering and prosperity, see part 6).

Deliverance from Satan's Power

ADAM AND EVE'S SIN not only brought about the curse of the Law, but also made them subject to Satan. As a result, Adam and Eve had to deal with spiritual assault from a dangerous and belligerent spiritual enemy. For the first time, Adam and Eve experienced fear, anxiety, depression, and despair. This frightful gamut of emotions was exactly part of what God meant when he said, "the day you eat of the fruit, you will surely die." Sin made us enemies of God **and** made us children of the devil. The apostle Paul wrote:

> ¹ And although you were dead in your transgressions and sins,
>
> ² in which you formerly lived according to this world's present path, according to the ruler of the kingdom of the air, **the ruler of the spirit that is now energizing the sons of disobedience,**
>
> Ephesians 2:1–2 (NET Bible)

Being under Satan's control means that, although man has a will and is capable of doing good things, ultimately man is subject to the devil who can bind, dominate, and destroy him.

The book of Job shows what Satan seeks to do to men who are in his power. Although Job was a believer, God allowed Satan to have limited access to work in Job's life. Satan afflicted Job with painful boils and sores, stole Job's wealth, and took the lives of his children. In fact, had God not prevented it, Satan would have taken Job's very life.

The afflictions of Satan are evident in the Gospels. During his earthly ministry, Jesus often healed and delivered people physically and mentally tormented by evil spirits. Sometimes, though not always, that physical torment involved physical illness (not everyone who is sick is under demonic oppression). Other times, it involved the spirits driving people to do things against their will, like cutting themselves or throwing themselves into fire.

Through the exorcisms that Jesus performed, Jesus went to war against the forces of darkness. Jesus drove out demons from their victims so often that the apostle Peter summarized the ministry of Jesus as follows:

> [38] how God anointed Jesus of Nazareth with the Holy Spirit and power, and how he went around **doing good and healing all who were under the power of the devil**, because God was with him.
>
> Acts 10:38 (NIV)

If we take that verse and put it together with the apostle John's observation:

> [19] We know that we are from God, and **the whole world lies in the power of the evil one**.
>
> 1 John 5:19 (ESV)

Then we can conclude that Satan has **power** over unsaved people, and that to be subject to Satan is to be subject to his affliction. This is one of the dreadful consequences of spiritual death.

The Cross of Christ Destroyed Satan's Power

The cross of Christ not only satisfied the judgment of God on our sin, but it also broke the power and dominion of Satan over our lives. Through Christ and his finished work, the Father disarmed principalities and powers, and openly defeated the devil and all the forces of darkness that had once been our master. Consider Colossians 2:14–15 in various translations:

> [14] by canceling the record of debt that stood against us with its legal demands. This he set aside, nailing it to the cross.
>
> [15] He **disarmed the rulers and authorities** and put them to open shame, by triumphing over them in him.
>
> Colossians 2:14-15 (ESV)

> [14] God wiped out the charges that were against us for disobeying the Law of Moses. He took them away and nailed them to the cross.
>
> [15] There **Christ defeated all powers and forces.** He let the whole world see them being led away as prisoners when he celebrated his victory.
>
> Colossians 2:14-15 (CEV)

> ¹⁴ having blotted out the handwriting in the ordinances that is against us, that was contrary to us, and he hath taken it out of the way, having nailed it to the cross;
>
> ¹⁵ **having stripped the principalities and the authorities, he made a shew of them openly—having triumphed over them in it.**
>
> Colossians 2:14-15 (YLT)

> Think of it! All sins forgiven, the slate wiped clean, that old arrest warrant canceled and nailed to Christ's cross. **He stripped all the spiritual tyrants in the universe of their sham authority at the Cross and marched them naked through the streets.**
>
> Colossians 2:14-15 (MSG)

By destroying the power of sin that held us in bondage, God **simultaneously** stopped the curse of the Law (called in Colossians 2 as the "record of debt that stood against us" or the "charges that were against us") from applying to us **and** obliterated the power of the devil over the Church. The only reason that Satan had control over man at all was because of sin, and by removing sin's power on the cross, Satan's source of control was destroyed. In plain vernacular, through Christ's crucifixion, the Father **whipped** the devil and **stripped** the demonic forces of all right of control or dominion that they held title to over the Church. Therefore, for the believer, Satan is a defeated foe. Because Satan attacks on a material, as well as a spiritual level, the victory of God at the cross was a victory over oppression and the attacks in both the spiritual and material areas of our lives. The Father has set the Church free over all the power of the enemy, and deliverance from Satan is the believer's inheritance.

Christ and the Church are Exalted Far Above Satan

Paul also writes that when God the Father raised Christ from the dead, Christ ascended to the right hand of the Father, "far above all rule and authority, power and dominion, and every title that can be given, not only in the present age but also in the one to come" (Ephesians 1: 20–21). All things have been put under Christ, who is the head over "every power and authority" (Colossians 2:10). The glory of Christ's resurrection is magnificently summed up in the following passage:

> ⁹ Therefore God has highly exalted him and bestowed on him the name that is above every name,
>
> ¹⁰ so that at the name of Jesus every knee should bow, in heaven and on earth and under the earth,
>
> ¹¹ and every tongue confess that Jesus Christ is Lord, to the glory of God the Father.
>
> Philippians 2:9–11 (ESV)

Christ is exalted above all human and spiritual power and authority, so that would obviously include Satan's kingdom. The believer is in Christ, and, therefore, is a partaker of Christ's exaltation (Ephesians 2:6).

Satan Still Rages Against the Church

Although Satan is a defeated foe, he is still a foe nonetheless. He remains a deceiver, and he directs the host of hell to war against the Church. I draw a lesson from American history to illustrate Satan's battle against the Church.

If you were of African descent living in America two hundred years ago, when slavery was permitted, you could have easily landed in a slave market. A violent and bloody civil war in America determined the course of slavery in the country. President Lincoln freed the slaves in the Confederate territories, and later, in defeating the Confederate army, he stripped slaveholders of their (questionable) legal right to keep human beings in bondage for their profit. Despite many years of being considered less than human, the US government elevated the freed slaves to having the same rights and privileges as any other American.

Sadly, the execution of emancipation was mishandled, and many freed slaves in the South finished in sharecropping arrangements that closely resembled slavery. Furthermore, after the Civil War, groups such as the Ku Klux Klan, as well as Jim Crow laws, reversed the gains of black Americans, and worked to keep them down and oppressed.

There is a tragic parallel here with the Church. God has set the Church free from Satan, and has given the Church all the rights and privileges as citizens of heaven with the authority to stop Satan. However, Satan has used illegal terror tactics against the Church, and sought to reverse her gains. Satan fights against the Church in many ways, and one way has been to afflict the Church with poverty and sickness. Poverty and sickness do not belong to us, but Satan stubbornly seeks to afflict us with it anyway, hoping that we will accept his calamities without resistance.

Satan the Thief

What evidence is there that Satan can affect us financially and physically? First, Jesus called Satan a liar and a thief (John 10:10). Jesus contrasted the work of Satan (to steal) with his work (to give abundant life). *Abundant life* means a prosperous, full, and satisfying life. If Christ came to give abundant life, then the devil must come to steal that abundance and give an impoverished life. He would seek to impose what is miserable, lacking, and unsatisfying. In addition, Satan would seek to deceive Christians into believing that God's abundance was not for them.

Someone said, *Well yes, but Jesus was talking about **spiritual things**. He wasn't talking about physical things like money.* Please refer to chapter 11, because there I explain that the spiritual and the physical realms are intertwined, but let us address that argument here as well.

Yes, Satan does steal spiritual things. He can steal the Word from people's hearts (Matthew 13:19). He can rob us of our joy, our peace, and our assurance of salvation. These are all spiritual things that the devil tries to steal from the Christian. The devil also steals spiritual things from non-Christians. Satan blinds the minds of unbelievers to prevent them from receiving the

Gospel, and he steals opportunities for people to hear the Gospel and be saved. However, the activity of Satan is not limited to the spiritual and unseen. We also see in the Gospel where Satan's work was to steal, physically and materially, from people. For example, the Gospels record how Satan stole health from people:

> [10] Now He was teaching in one of the synagogues on the Sabbath.
>
> [11] And behold, there was a woman who had **a spirit of infirmity eighteen years**, and was bent over and could in no way raise herself up.
>
> [12] But when Jesus saw her, He called her to Him and said to her, "Woman, you are loosed from your infirmity."
>
> [13] And He laid His hands on her, and immediately she was made straight, and glorified God.
>
> [14] But the ruler of the synagogue, indignant because Jesus had healed on the Sabbath, said to the people, "There are six days in which work ought to be done. Come on those days and be healed, and not on the Sabbath day."
>
> [15] The Lord then answered him and said, "Hypocrite! Does not each one of you on the Sabbath loose his ox or donkey from the stall, and lead it away to water it?
>
> [16] So ought not this woman, being a daughter of Abraham, **whom Satan has bound**—think of it—for eighteen years, be loosed from this bond on the Sabbath?"
>
> Luke 13:10–16 (NKJV)

A spirit of infirmity is a demonic power whose assignment is to make people sick. This foul spirit afflicted this poor woman, causing her to be stooped over for eighteen years and literally stole her physical health.

Deliverance from Satan's Power

When Satan attacks the physical health of a person, he attacks that person's prosperity on every level. When Satan caused this woman to be stooped over for eighteen years, he stole her ability to work and be productive in a normal fashion. He stole the pleasure of normal family relations, and the money that could have been used for other things went to doctors who could not cure the affliction.

Jesus makes it clear that the woman was not suffering for righteousness' sake. Nor was she suffering because she had done something wrong. She was suffering because Satan had kept her bound. Jesus implies that this woman being bound was a violation of the Abrahamic covenant when he says, "this daughter of Abraham." In other words, Satan illegally afflicted that woman and caused her to suffer for eighteen years. Note that Jesus healed her instantly. He would not tolerate her suffering, not one moment more!

There is a difference between judgment and satanic affliction, so it is important to have understanding in these areas. For example, even Christ's disciples made the error of judging a circumstance of illness to be a form of God's punishment:

> [1] As he passed by, he saw a man blind from birth.
>
> [2] And his disciples asked him, "Rabbi, who sinned, this man or his parents, that he was born blind?"
>
> [3] Jesus answered, "It was not that this man sinned, or his parents, but that the works of God might be displayed in him.
>
> [4] We must work the works of him who sent me while it is day; night is coming, when no one can work.

> ⁵ As long as I am in the world, I am the light of the world."
>
> John 9:1–5 (ESV)

Given their understanding of the Scriptures, the disciples' question was a perfectly reasonable one. Sickness was a curse that came upon sinners. However, Jesus said that their understanding of sin did not apply in this situation. The man's blindness was an occasion to show forth the power of God. People can suffer for reasons unrelated to their sins, and the only thing that will reverse their suffering is the work of the Holy Spirit through the Church.

Besides causing sickness, the influence of Satan can also create a direct assault on the believer's finances. For example, the Israelites' bondage in Egypt was a picture of how satanic oppression includes financial devastation:

> ¹¹ Therefore they set taskmasters over them to afflict them with heavy burdens. They built for Pharaoh store cities, Pithom and Raamses.
>
> ¹² But the more they were oppressed, the more they multiplied and the more they spread abroad. And the Egyptians were in dread of the people of Israel.
>
> ¹³ So they ruthlessly made the people of Israel work as slaves
>
> ¹⁴ and made their lives bitter with hard service, in mortar and brick, and in all kinds of work in the field. In all their work they ruthlessly made them work as slaves.
>
> Exodus 1:11–14 (ESV)

The Israelites had been an abundant and successful people in Egypt. They had come to Egypt through the influence of Joseph and they prospered under the protection of Pharaoh who knew and trusted Joseph. However, when there was a change in leadership, the Israelites no longer had favor. The new dynasty enslaved and oppressed the Israelites. God's people were completely disfranchised and stripped of their prosperity. The desperate plight of the Israelites shows Satan's plan for God's people. **The devil is insistent on keeping God's people poor and in despair.**

One of the first things that God did when liberating the children of Israel was to make them rich. The devil stole Israel's wealth and transferred it to Pharaoh, but God reversed that by transferring the wealth of the Egyptians into the hands of the Israelites.

As noted with Job, when Job was out from under the protection of God, one of the first things the devil did was to impoverish him. Although the devil stole from Job and caused immense suffering, God turned the tables. The Bible says:

> [10] And the LORD restored the fortunes of Job, when he had prayed for his friends. And the LORD gave Job twice as much as he had before.
>
> Job 42:10 (ESV)

In the New Testament, Satan continues to financially hinder God's people in various ways. The writer of Hebrews writes to believers who had suffered the wrath of the enemy:

> [32] But recall the former days when, after you were enlightened, you endured a hard struggle with sufferings,
>
> [33] sometimes being publicly exposed to reproach and affliction, and sometimes being partners with those so treated.

> ³⁴ For you had compassion on those in prison, **and you joyfully accepted the plundering of your property**, since you knew that you yourselves had a better possession and an abiding one.
>
> Hebrews 10:32–34 (ESV)

These Christians suffered because of their faith in God, and suffered at the hands of people whom Satan was influencing. Part of what they suffered was the confiscation of their property, and a direct attack on their financial prosperity.

These are just a few scriptural examples that illustrate that Satan steals money from God's people.

Satan is not the sole cause of every problem in life that is experienced by Christians, financial or otherwise. However, too often, Christians tend to ignore the fact that principalities and powers fight against them in the financial realm. The tendency is to address money problems exclusively through natural means, such as budgeting or investing. Although these kinds of steps are effective and important, they will not stop a spiritual attack.

The apostles understood the activity of demons and how to defeat them. For example:

> ⁸ Be sober-minded; be watchful. Your adversary the devil prowls around like a roaring lion, seeking someone to devour.
>
> ⁹ **Resist him, firm in your faith**, knowing that the same kinds of suffering are being experienced by your brotherhood throughout the world.
>
> 1 Peter 5:8–9 (ESV)

Deliverance from Satan's Power

> ⁷ Submit yourselves therefore to God. **Resist the devil, and he will flee from you.**
>
> James 4:7 (ESV)

Although he is a dangerous foe, believers can stop the work of the enemy. Note that Peter did not say, *Pray that Jesus would resist the devil for you.* No, the Church has been redeemed from Satan and given authority from Christ to resist him on the earth. If we sin, then we can receive forgiveness immediately and close the door to judgment or the affliction of Satan. When we abide in Christ, we can know that God will allow our faith to be tested, but he will not curse us.

If we think **God** is making us sick and making us poor, we will accept the sickness and the poverty, and we **will not** have faith to be healed or delivered. If we are in fellowship with God, and understand what it means to be redeemed from the curse of the Law, and how Christ already bore the penalty of our sins, then we will not waste a moment thinking that God is putting curses on us. The penalty for our sins has already been paid! Similarly, by understanding our redemption from the dominion of darkness, we will understand that Satan no longer has a legal right to afflict us. He once had the authority to oppress us, but now Satan is under our feet. When we start to experience poverty, we can resist the enemy and he will flee from us. This is our inheritance in Christ. In the next two chapters, we will look more closely at the nature of our inheritance in Christ.

The Superiority of Our Inheritance

REDEMPTION INVOLVES THE FORGIVENESS of sin and deliverance from the kingdom of darkness. Redemption is the Church's inheritance and is a **spiritual** reality:

> ³ Blessed be the God and Father of our Lord Jesus Christ! According to his great mercy, he has caused us to be born again to a living hope through the resurrection of Jesus Christ from the dead,
>
> ⁴ to an inheritance that is imperishable, undefiled, and unfading, kept in heaven for you,
>
> ⁵ who by God's power are being guarded through faith for a salvation ready to be revealed in the last time.
>
> 1 Peter 1:3–5 (ESV)

> ¹⁸ knowing that you were ransomed from the futile ways inherited from your forefathers, not with perishable things such as silver or gold,
>
> ¹⁹ but with the precious blood of Christ, like that of a lamb without blemish or spot.
>
> 1 Peter 1:18–19 (ESV)

Our inheritance is not a commodity that money can buy. Our inheritance in Christ is a spiritual, heavenly reality that comes to us through spiritual means; that is, faith in the shed blood of Christ. The phrase "kept in heaven" is translated as "reserved in heaven" in the King James Version, and in the Greek, it means *attend to carefully, to take care of,* also to *guard*.[14] God the Father is carefully maintaining and preserving our inheritance in heaven, and, therefore, our inheritance in Christ is unaffected by what happens on the earth. Our inheritance in Christ has implications in this life and in the life to come. Even though our inheritance is spiritual, we may begin to enjoy our redemption now in this life:

> [10] I have come that they may have life, and that they may have it more abundantly.
>
> John 10:10b (NKJV)

The abundant life of salvation does not begin after we die. We can benefit from the remission of sins now. We can experience the peace of God now. We can walk in God's wisdom in this life. The moment a person confesses Jesus as Lord, he experiences salvation in real time. The Scripture says:

> [17] Therefore, if anyone is in Christ, he is a new creation. The old has passed away; behold, the new has come.
>
> 2 Corinthians 5:17 (ESV)

This is a blessed truth. As believers, **once we** were sinners by nature, but now we are children of God in Christ. Through redemption, the believer is made immeasurably spiritually prosperous, and our spiritual inheritance in Christ will never lose its value, never be diminished, and never be found insufficient or lacking at all.

Often, people worry whether they will have enough provision when they get old. Will their money last? Will their families be there to care for them? Believers have no equivalent concern about their salvation. Our spiritual riches in Christ will never run out. As believers, we will never come to the end of God's grace. Christ has accomplished a complete and finished work for his Church!

The spiritual aspect of our inheritance must be foundational to the believer's thinking to receive material prosperity because:

- Spiritual things are greater than natural things, and spiritual processes are greater than natural processes.
- Spiritual realities have an impact, and influence the natural realities (natural objects, circumstances, and conditions).

The Spirit and the Natural

Because our inheritance in Christ is a spiritual reality, let us examine the biblical use of the terms *spiritual* and *natural* more carefully.

Various religious traditions completely separate the spiritual and natural worlds. However, the biblical view is that, although the spirit and the natural are distinct, they are not

exclusive. Spiritual and natural things are different in terms of their origin and how there are perceived. Spiritual things (and in this instance, I mean *divine* things) come from heaven, and natural things originate in the earth. We perceive natural things using our five physical senses (touch, taste, smell, hearing, sight). Spiritual things refer to what is beyond the grasp of our senses. We cannot see the throne of God, but it exists. We cannot touch angels, but they are encamped around the believer. Outside of divine intervention, man cannot perceive the spirit realm though it exists.

One exception to this basic distinction is that, although the realm of Satan and demons is also spiritual, Scripture often groups demonic activity with what is worldly and carnal (Galatians 5:16ff, James 3:13ff, Romans 8:7). Therefore, *natural*, *physical*, or *material* may refer to common physical objects, manufactured systems, or that originating from Satan. We see this distinction of origin when the Apostles wrote about wisdom:

> [21] For when the world with all its **earthly wisdom** failed to perceive and recognize and know God by means of its own philosophy, God in **His wisdom** was pleased through the foolishness of preaching [salvation, procured by Christ and to be had through Him], to save those who believed (who clung to and trusted in and relied on Him).
>
> 1 Corinthians 1:21 (Amplified)

> [13] Who is wise and understanding among you? Let them show it by their good life, by deeds done in the humility that comes from wisdom.

> ¹⁴ But if you harbor bitter envy and selfish ambition in your hearts, do not boast about it or deny the truth.
>
> ¹⁵ **Such "wisdom" does not come down from heaven but is earthly, unspiritual, demonic.**
>
> ¹⁶ For where you have envy and selfish ambition, there you find disorder and every evil practice.
>
> ¹⁷ But the **wisdom that comes from heaven** is first of all pure; then peace-loving, considerate, submissive, full of mercy and good fruit, impartial and sincere.
>
> James 3:13–17 (NIV)

There is a spiritual, divine, or heavenly wisdom, and then there is an earthly, unspiritual, and devilish wisdom. Although both are indeed forms of wisdom, their origin is of great significance.

The Interaction of the Spirit and the Natural

Despite their distinctions, there is continuing interaction between the spiritual and the natural worlds, and spiritual forces **constantly** influence the natural world. In this sense, spiritual and natural things are not separate, but intertwined.

The creation account in Genesis records the prime example of how the spiritual affected the natural. The earth was formless and empty, and the Spirit of God hovered over the waters. Now when God said, "light be" the natural, material world changed, as the universe was flooded with light. The spiritual power of the Word of God transformed the unformed and void in the natural into something good and beautiful. Although that good and perfect world became corrupt through sin, God continued to intervene in the physical world. Jacobs's dream about angels descending from heaven to the earth and ascending from the earth to heaven is a vivid picture of the constant interaction between the divine world and the material world:

> [12] And he dreamed that there was a ladder set up on the earth, and the top of it reached to heaven; and the angels of God were ascending and descending on it!
>
> [13] And behold, the Lord stood over and beside him and said, I am the Lord, the God of Abraham your father [forefather] and the God of Isaac; I will give to you and to your descendants the land on which you are lying.
>
> Genesis 28:12–13 (Amplified)

From a divine perspective, God intervenes and manifests his spiritual glory in the earth for our good. The angels of God were not ascending and descending to get exercise. They were carrying out the will of God on the earth, in this case, the fulfillment of God's promise to Abraham.

The Incarnation is perhaps the ultimate example of how the spiritual can manifest in the natural world. The apostle John wrote:

> [1] In the beginning was the Word, and the Word was with God, and the Word was God.
>
> [2] He was in the beginning with God.
>
> [14] And the Word became flesh and dwelt among us, and we beheld His glory, the glory as of the only begotten of the Father, full of grace and truth.
>
> John 1:1–2, 14 (NKJV)

Although the Word was spiritual and divine, he became flesh and manifested in the natural realm. Christ was the perfect expression of God's will manifested in the natural, physical realm.

The Superiority of the Spirit Over the Natural

Spiritual things existed before natural things and spiritual things are far more durable. For example, the apostle Paul contrasted the natural body with the spiritual body. He taught that the natural body is weak and perishable, but the spiritual body is powerful and glorious (1 Corinthians 15:42-44).

The dominant nature of the supernatural is evident also in the ministry of Christ (the Word made flesh):

- He dominated sickness and disease.
- He exercised authority over demonic power, and drove out demons that controlled people.
- He demonstrated superiority over false religions and the wisdom of men.
- The very forces of nature, including death itself, bowed before Christ.

We can think of the miracles of Jesus (and indeed, all the miracles of the Bible), as divinely overriding the natural order. For example, when Jesus walked on water, he was overriding the natural laws of physics and gravity that would have normally made such an act impossible.

The miracles of Jesus not only prove the superiority of the divine over what is physical, but they also show the will of God. Jesus said:

> ¹⁰ Do you not believe that I am in the Father and the Father is in me? The words that I say to you I do not speak on my own authority, but the Father who dwells in me does his works.
> ¹¹ Believe me that I am in the Father and the Father is in me, or else believe on account of the works themselves.
>
> John 14:10-11 (ESV)

Jesus' miracles proved his message, and proved that Jesus was doing God's will. More precisely, the miracles of Jesus showed us that God wanted to bring his power into the lives of people for their good—even when they were without hope. When Jesus healed the sick, it proved God's intention to heal even those incurably ill. When Jesus drove out demons, it expressed God's intention to bring deliverance to people beyond the reach of human aid.

The exercise of divine spiritual power is always in line with divine spiritual purpose. When spiritual things manifest apart from the holy will and purpose of God, that manifestation is ultimately demonic.

In the next chapter, we will see how the dominant nature of our spiritual inheritance benefits the Church in the natural realm.

The Authority of Our Inheritance

INDISPUTABLY, JESUS CHRIST IS unique. He is the chief cornerstone. There is no other name under heaven by which men might be saved. He alone accomplished the Father's great plan of redemption and he alone is the image of the invisible God, the firstborn of all creation. However, in our earnestness to maintain the Lord Jesus in his rightful place, we must not deny the fullness of what he provided to the Church. The miracles of Jesus not only verified his divinity and authenticated his message, but they also served as a model for how God wants to operate **through the Church.** They showed that God intends to manifest his divine glory through **people** whom Christ redeemed. Indeed, Jesus taught that his followers would do the works he did after he returned to the Father:

> [12] "Truly, truly, I say to you, whoever believes in me will also do the works that I do; and greater works than these will he do, because I am going to the Father.
>
> John 14:12 (ESV)

God intended for the dominion and authority of heaven to manifest through believers. Our inheritance in Christ includes citizenship in Christ's kingdom (Colossians 1:13), and with this citizenship comes rights and privileges reserved for the believer.

The Church has focused on some rights of the believers, but has neglected others. For example, Christians are taught typically about the right and privilege of receiving the continuing forgiveness of sins and purification from unrighteousness (1 John 1:9), or the right to be guided and directed by the Holy Spirit (John 16:12–13).

However, Jesus also has given to the Church the privilege and the license to perform works in his name. For example, in his earthly ministry, Jesus conferred authority to his twelve disciples:

> [1] And he called to him his twelve disciples and gave them authority over unclean spirits, to cast them out, and to heal every disease and every affliction.
>
> Matthew 10:1 (ESV)

Jesus did not limit this power to the Twelve. He also gave his authority to others:

> [1] After this the Lord appointed seventy-two others and sent them on ahead of him, two by two, into every town and place where he himself was about to go.
>
> [17] The seventy-two returned with joy, saying, "Lord, even the demons are subject to us in your name!"
>
> Luke 10:1, 17 (ESV)

The Authority of Our Inheritance

The intent of God to manifest his power on the earth was so strong that even those not explicitly part of Jesus' entourage were able to perform works of power in his name:

> [49] John answered, "Master, we saw someone casting out demons in your name, and we tried to stop him, because he does not follow with us."
>
> [50] But Jesus said to him, "Do not stop him, for the one who is not against you is for you."
>
> Luke 9:49–50 (ESV)

Jesus reiterated that he had given the Church license to use his name and authority on his behalf before he ascended to the Father:

> [18] And Jesus came and said to them, "All authority in heaven and on earth has been given to me.
>
> Matthew 28:18 (ESV)

> [15] And he said to them, "Go into all the world and proclaim the gospel to the whole creation.
>
> [16] Whoever believes and is baptized will be saved, but whoever does not believe will be condemned.
>
> [17] And these signs will accompany those who believe: in my name they will cast out demons; they will speak in new tongues;
>
> [18] they will pick up serpents with their hands; and if they drink any deadly poison, it will not hurt them; they will lay their hands on the sick, and they will recover."
>
> Mark 16:15–18 (ESV)

The mandate to use Jesus' name is for both the believer individually and the Church corporately.

Our Inheritance Includes the Power of God

Jesus not only gave the Church his name, but he also empowered the Church to do God's work on the earth (Acts 1:7–8). Both the authority of Christ and the power of God are part of the **spiritual inheritance** that the Father gave us when he made us alive in Christ and transferred us into his kingdom. Christ's empowerment of individual believers to do his work was so significant that Paul prayed that God the Father would open the eyes of the Church to this reality, praying that the Father would help us understand "the immeasurable greatness of his power toward us who believe" (Ephesians 1:19).

When Paul wrote about the exceedingly great power of God available to the believer, he was only echoing what Jesus taught his disciples. Jesus gave his followers a glimpse of what they could do if they learned how to wield the power of God:

> [20] *As they passed by in the morning, they saw the fig tree withered away to its roots.*
>
> [21] *And Peter remembered and said to him, "Rabbi, look! The fig tree that you cursed has withered."*
>
> [22] *And Jesus answered them, "Have faith in God.*
>
> [23] *Truly, I say to you, whoever says to this mountain, 'Be taken up and thrown into the sea,' and does not doubt in his heart, but believes that what he says will come to pass, it will be done for him.*

The Authority of Our Inheritance

> [24] Therefore I tell you, whatever you ask in prayer, believe that you have received it, and it will be yours.
>
> Mark 11:20–24 (ESV)

Jesus spoke to a fig tree, and the fig tree dried up from the roots and withered within a twenty-four-hour period. Peter excitedly noted the miracle, and Jesus immediately used the opportunity to teach the fact that individual believers could apply spiritual forces in the earthly realm (such as faith) to get the results they desire (that these desires must be in line with God's will is implied).

Jesus' mastery over the fig tree and subsequent teaching on faith illustrates a profound spiritual truth. The believer's authority not only applies to the realm of Christian service and ministry, but also to the realm of our personal needs.

Professional religionists often make the Church laity out to be a gang of rogues and suspects who will abuse the power of God for selfish ends at every chance they get. For that reason, these self-appointed deputies are always conjuring up excuses of why the power of God will not work for the believer. However, Christ's unconditional conferral of spiritual authority on the **entire Church** proves God's implicit confidence in all his children. God expects us to grow up in Him, and to think as he thinks, talk as he talks, and do the works that he would do. The Father has boldly given the Church the keys to his kingdom, to operate spiritual principles to get their needs met, and to be a blessing on the earth. Consider God's confidence in the believer, indicated in Jesus' teaching on faith:

> [24] Therefore I say unto you, What things soever **ye desire**, when ye pray, believe that ye receive them, and ye shall have them.
>
> Mark 11:24 (KJV)

The Father desires to meet all our needs according to his riches in glory in Christ Jesus, that is, our inheritance in Christ, and he has commanded his people to ask him for what we want.

Without spiritual authority and power, believers would only experience our inheritance in Christ by direct, sovereign acts of God. However, God, in his wisdom, has given the Church permission to manifest, intentionally and discretionally, his power **to bless the world and themselves.** Of course, because the Church can do nothing without Christ, I am not talking about people running around trying to do things without faith and direction from God. However, according to the Word of God, I can do anything that the Word says I can do, and I can have anything that the Word says I can have. This exercise of our authority extends to the area of financial prosperity.

The believer's inheritance in Christ is spiritual in nature, and, therefore, cannot decay, be stolen, or otherwise perish. Believers can use their inheritance now in this life to bless themselves and be a blessing to others. The next section examines the financial aspect of our inheritance.

PART 5
CONTRASTING DIVINE WEALTH AND WORLDLY WEALTH

Defining Divine Wealth

FINANCIAL WEALTH IS AN integral part of God's covenant to Abraham. All the promises and blessings that Abraham enjoyed, including financial wealth, became known as *the blessing of Abraham* and were inherited by his son, his grandson, and even a nation of millions. Finally, the exalted Jesus of Nazareth became the consummate heir of the blessing of Abraham. Through Christ's finished work, the Church has become the seed of Abraham and the inheritor of the blessing of Abraham. In this section, we will look at 2 Corinthians 8 and 9 to determine a more granular definition of financial prosperity.

Chapters 8 and 9 of 2 Corinthians contain the longest dissertation on financial prosperity in the New Testament. In these Scriptures, Paul is teaching on money by referring to the Corinthian churches' commitment to send financial offerings to the saints in Jerusalem. He explains the benefits that will accrue to them if they follow through on that commitment. Paul's exposition on the biblical principles of financial blessing provides one of the most thorough definitions of divine prosperity in the New Testament:

> ⁶ Remember this: Whoever sows sparingly will also reap sparingly, and whoever sows generously will also reap generously.
>
> ⁷ Each of you should give what you have decided in your heart to give, not reluctantly or under compulsion, for God loves a cheerful giver.
>
> ⁸ And God is able to bless you abundantly, so that in all things at all times, having all that you need, you will abound in every good work.
>
> ⁹ As it is written:
> "They have freely scattered their gifts to the poor;
> their righteousness endures forever."
>
> ¹⁰ Now he who supplies seed to the sower and bread for food will also supply and increase your store of seed and will enlarge the harvest of your righteousness.
>
> ¹¹ You will be enriched in every way so that you can be generous on every occasion, and through us your generosity will result in thanksgiving to God.
>
> 2 Corinthians 9:6–11 (NIV)

Paul explains that:

- God prospers us so we can meet our own needs abundantly.
- God prospers us so we can finance God's work.

This definition is so complete as to end the argument. Biblical wealth could never be misconstrued as selfish materialism, because part of its intrinsic purpose is to meet the needs of others.

It could never be dismissed as impractical, because it accounts for the real, everyday needs of the believer.

However, Paul's definition of being rich does not correspond to a specific income level or monetary amount. The focus of divine prosperity is not the sum acquired, but the enablement of believers to take care of their affairs and be a blessing to others.

Divine Prosperity to Meet Our Needs

According to Paul, one reason that God prospers us is to meet our needs, therefore, it is important to define *needs*.

Most people typically think about needs and desires differently because of financial lack. People need clothes but want designer fashions; they need a place to live but want an impressive house. Even in the most mundane situations, people are constantly settling for less than they desire because they do not have enough money. If I am short on cash, I go to the fast-food chain and order lunch from the $1 menu. When payday comes, however, I drive past the fast-food restaurant to get the meal that I really want.

When I was in fourth grade, I stopped by a friend's house on the way to school. He was in the kitchen preparing lunch, and two things stick out in my memory. First, when he opened the refrigerator, I saw that it was stocked full of food. Second, when my friend asked his mom what kind of sandwich he should make, she yelled from another room, *Bologna! And only take one slice.* Sure enough, he made his sandwich with exactly one slice of bologna (and a microscopic amount of mayonnaise). After all these years, that was still the loneliest sandwich I have ever seen!

Many Christians see God as the God who owns the cattle on a thousand hills, but who will only give them a meager sandwich when they are hungry. Many think, *God will meet my needs, but not my wants. I have to get my wants on my own.* However, the apostle Paul presents God as the God who meets our needs richly and abundantly. His provision is so abundant in fact that once our needs are met, there will be plenty left over to contribute to the needs of others. It is difficult for Christians to internalize and really believe this, because we have been trained to not trust our wants.

Some desires are wrong. However, Jesus taught that his followers have license to not only desire things, but also to expect God to fulfill those desires, precisely because the Father wants to meet our desires. Christ said:

> [24] Therefore I say unto you, What things soever **ye desire**, when ye pray, believe that ye receive them, and ye shall have them.
>
> Mark 11:24 (KJV)

> [23] And in that day ye shall ask me nothing. Verily, verily, I say unto you, **Whatsoever ye shall ask the Father in my name, he will give it you.**
>
> John 16:23 (KJV)

God does not have an issue with meeting our needs **or** our desires. However, God commands his children not to be greedy and he will not satisfy the desires of the covetous. This is the heavenly bifurcation: godly desires as opposed to ungodly desires, and temperance as opposed to greed. If God commands his children not to be covetous, yet promises to meet our needs and desires, then it is possible for believers to pray *greed free* and get what they need and want from heaven.

Wealth to Preach the Gospel

The second reason that God wants us to be rich is so we can be generous every time and abound in every good work. By good works, Paul means to finance the ministry of the Gospel whether by supporting preachers, giving to the poor or funding ministry projects. Paul's teaching drives home the point that God's work requires money, and second, it is the responsibility of the Church to finance the preaching of the Gospel.

God's Work Requires Money

God has called people into the ministry who need training and he has called Christian organizations to be a blessing to society. Fulfilling this calling requires money. Anyone who is involved in Christian work knows that lack of money is a major hindrance to the spreading of the Gospel. If God's people are financially wanting, then the ministries that they are called to support will be lacking as well.

Some might say, *Well, as Christians, we don't need to be rich. We just need to better manage what we already have, and not spend as much. If everyone does his or her part, there will be enough. A lot of little offerings will add up over time.*

This kind of thinking has held the Church back for centuries. First, it limits God, who has revealed himself as El Shaddai ("God Almighty," see Exodus 6:3).

Second, this kind of thinking severely underestimates the urgent need for the Church to be active on the earth. Ministry needs are so great globally it will take an **entire army** to evangelize and minister to people, and it will take a large sum to get this job done.

In 2003, the US led a multinational force against Iraq as part of the US war on terror. Although the US and its allies were militarily superior to Iraq, the US commanders organized an invading force of thousands of troops and overwhelming firepower to subdue the Iraqi army. The financial expense to deploy this army and subdue the enemy was enormous. Even after the old Iraqi regime was deposed and a new government established, the US and its allies continued to spend billions of dollars to stabilize the country.

When it comes to war, the US and its allies understand that it takes a hard-to-believe sum of money and resources to win a war and keep the peace. Yet the US government will spare no expense to achieve its wartime objectives. The US has learned that the best military victory must be decisive.

Defining Divine Wealth

Some in the Church, in contrast, want to go to war against the forces of darkness on the cheap. God has promised abundant prosperity to train ministers, establish churches, build hospitals, distribute medicines, build orphanages, feed the hungry, and broadcast the Gospel over every medium possible. However, some in the Church want to say, *Lord, we know it takes money to do your work, but we don't want to ask for too much. Just give us a little bit, and we'll learn how to manage.*

No, God wants to make the Church rich, so the Church will have her needs met then support the work of God abundantly.

Old Testament Examples of Financing God's Work

Throughout Scripture, God has called on his people to support, and fund his work. His typical method of doing this was to bless his people with physical resources, then call on them to willingly give part of those resources to finance his work. There are many examples of this in Scripture, but one of the most vivid examples is in the book of Exodus. The Scripture recounts how the people of God were slaves to a cruel and unyielding dictator (Exodus 1:8–14). However, although Pharaoh was oppressing the Israelites, the Lord had a reparation plan in mind for his people:

> [35] The Israelites did as Moses instructed and asked the Egyptians for articles of silver and gold and for clothing.
>
> [36] The LORD had made the Egyptians favorably disposed toward the people, and they gave them what they asked for; **so they plundered the Egyptians.**
>
> Exodus 12:35–36 (ESV)

Exodus records an amazing transference of wealth from one nation to another without a single sword being raised. The children of Israel, at the command of the Lord, asked their oppressors for their wealth and the Egyptians urgently gave them whatever they asked.

The Exodus incident is also recalled in the Psalms:

> 37 He brought out Israel, laden with silver and gold, and from among their tribes no one faltered.
>
> Psalms 105:37 (NIV)

The children of Israel left Egypt laden with valuable treasures. The word *laden* means to carry a heavy load. In modern vernacular, we refer to a rich person as being *loaded*. Well, the Israelites, who had been slaves, were now leaving their captivity *loaded*. They were not leaving Egypt with a few coins, a mule, and a sack of potatoes. The Israelites were carrying loads **heavy** with silver and gold. In a masterstroke, God had made his people wealthy. This is divine prosperity, and this prosperity involved financial gain. However, that was not the end of the story, as God would later call on Israel to contribute some of that wealth to build a place of worship:

> 1 The LORD said to Moses,
>
> 2 "Speak to the people of Israel, that they take for me a contribution. From every man whose heart moves him you shall receive the contribution for me.
>
> 3 And this is the contribution that you shall receive from them: gold, silver, and bronze,

Defining Divine Wealth

> ⁴ blue and purple and scarlet yarns and fine twined linen, goats' hair,
>
> ⁵ tanned rams' skins, goatskins, acacia wood,
>
> ⁶ oil for the lamps, spices for the anointing oil and for the fragrant incense,
>
> ⁷ onyx stones, and stones for setting, for the ephod and for the breastpiece.
>
> ⁸ And let them make me a sanctuary, that I may dwell in their midst.
>
> Exodus 25:1–8 (ESV)

When the Lord called on Moses to build the Tabernacle in the wilderness, he instructed Moses to take up an offering to be willingly offered by the people of God. He specifically commanded Moses to receive gold and silver. Now, from where would two to three million emancipated slaves out in the wilderness get gold and silver? From where would they get rare oils, spices, linens, and hides of sea cows? This came from the wealth transferred to them from the Egyptians.

We can see from the story of the Exodus that God gave his people money and valuables–lots of it! We have to get out of our minds the thinking that God wants his children to be broke. If God wanted Israel poor, he would not have given them gold and silver. God gave the children of Israel money so their needs could be supplied **and** so they could give generously to the work of God.

The Example of Hezekiah

Let us look at another example. When Hezekiah, the king of Judah, set out to purify the temple and restore a proper worship of God in the land, he gave an order for the citizens to support this work financially. Although some Israelites scoffed at Hezekiah's intentions, many people responded to God's leader and brought in their tithes and offerings to ensure that the ministers could be devoted to the Lord:

> [4] And he commanded the people who lived in Jerusalem to give the portion due to the priests and the Levites, that they might give themselves to the Law of the LORD.
>
> [5] As soon as the command was spread abroad, the people of Israel gave in abundance the firstfruits of grain, wine, oil, honey, and of all the produce of the field. And they brought in abundantly the tithe of everything.
>
> [6] And the people of Israel and Judah who lived in the cities of Judah also brought in the tithe of cattle and sheep, and the tithe of the dedicated things that had been dedicated to the LORD their God, and laid them in heaps.
>
> [7] In the third month they began to pile up the heaps, and finished them in the seventh month.
>
> [8] When Hezekiah and the princes came and saw the heaps, they blessed the LORD and his people Israel.
>
> [9] And Hezekiah questioned the priests and the Levites about the heaps.
>
> [10] Azariah the chief priest, who was of the house of Zadok, answered him, "Since they began to bring the contributions into the house of the LORD, we have eaten

Defining Divine Wealth

> and had enough and have plenty left, for the LORD has blessed his people, so that we have this large amount left."
>
> 2 Chronicles 31:4-10 (ESV)

There is no question that this passage is talking about money and physical goods to meet the material needs of the ministry. The people of God gave so much that their contributions began to pile up in heaps in the temple. There was so much income that Hezekiah wondered where all the money was coming from! Why were the people of God able to give like that? The chief priest answered, "because the Lord has blessed his people."

In other words, God had made the Israelites so wealthy that when they gave a tithe of their income (a tithe is ten percent) to the temple, the offerings began to pile up. There was enough provision to abundantly support an entire division of priests and Levites.

If the Israelites had been poor, subsistence farmers, eking out a living and barely getting by, a tithe of their income would not have gone very far. It would not have piled up in heaps in the temple, and the priest and Levites would not have been able to minister full-time. As a result, the order of worship that God intended to re-establish in the earth would have been wanting.

This example further illustrates the pattern God has set forth for funding his enterprises in the earth. He blesses an obedient people financially, enabling them to both meet their own needs and to have plenty left over to give generously into his work. What is astonishing is that the abundance was realized in four months. It does not take years and years for God to move.

New Testament Examples of Financing God's Work

The New Testament principles of giving and receiving echo the principles of the Old Testament. Just as God gave the nation Israel the privilege of supporting God's work, so God gives this privilege to the Body of Christ.

Christ himself was supported by the freewill contributions of others. Jesus was not a part-time preacher who supported himself with carpentry jobs. He worked as a carpenter, but after being anointed by God and launched into the ministry, he received support from others:

> [40] Some women were watching from a distance. Among them were Mary Magdalene, Mary the mother of James the younger and of Joseph, and Salome.
>
> [41] In Galilee these women had followed him and cared for his needs. Many other women who had come up with him to Jerusalem were also there.
>
> Mark 15:40–41 (NIV)

Obviously, Christ did not need the women's support. A man who could feed five-thousand people from a small boy's lunch, who could turn water into wine, or retrieve tax money from the mouth of a fish did not need anything from anyone. Christ **allowed** his followers the privilege of giving into his ministry because this was consistent with the principles of Scripture. Christ also extended the right to receive support to the Twelve:

Defining Divine Wealth

> ⁵ These twelve Jesus sent out, instructing them, "Go nowhere among the Gentiles and enter no town of the Samaritans,
>
> ⁶ but go rather to the lost sheep of the house of Israel.
>
> ⁷ And proclaim as you go, saying, 'The kingdom of heaven is at hand.'
>
> ⁸ Heal the sick, raise the dead, cleanse lepers, cast out demons. You received without paying; give without pay.
>
> ⁹ Acquire no gold nor silver nor copper for your belts,
>
> ¹⁰ no bag for your journey, nor two tunics nor sandals nor a staff, **for the laborer deserves his food.**
>
> ¹¹ And whatever town or village you enter, find out who is worthy in it **and stay there until you depart.**
>
> Matthew 10:5-11 (ESV)

Jesus sent out his Apostles with clear instructions that they were to receive food, lodging and provision from the people to whom they were sent. They were forbidden to charge fees for their ministry, but were expected to receive offerings to meet their needs.

People often take the phrase "acquire no gold nor silver nor copper" out of context. Christ was not saying that his Apostles had to wander around flat broke, with no money in their pockets, begging on a street corner for their next meal. He was not saying that they could only have one set of clothes. If we were to interpret that Scripture to mean that, then it would be wrong for a minister to own more than one set of clothes, or have money in her purse! The Twelve were, in a sense, like the priests and Levites of the Old Testament. They were presiding over the building of a new and living temple known as the Body of Christ. The Lord did not want them to have one foot in a secular enterprise and one foot in the ministry. Therefore, he commanded them to draw their living from the people who received their ministry. Christ was continuing a tradition first recorded in the Old Testament: that the people of God should financially support the ministry.

Just as the preaching of the Gospel would be extended beyond the original Apostles of Christ, so would the command for God's people to support the ministry. The apostle Paul reiterates this commandment in 1 Corinthians:

> [13] Do you not know that those who are employed in the temple service get their food from the temple, and those who serve at the altar share in the sacrificial offerings?
>
> [14] In the same way, the Lord commanded that those who proclaim the gospel should get their living by the gospel.
>
> 1 Corinthians 9:13–14 (ESV)

In this verse, the altar that Paul is referring to is the altar in the temple where the Israelites gave their offerings. When the Israelites came with their bulls, or goats, or grain, the priests received their tithes and offerings and presented them to the Lord. After the necessary ceremonies, they distributed what was left over to the priests, serving at the altar, to bring home to their families. Paul is linking the giving of tithes and offerings in the Old Testament to the obligations of believers under the New Testament. The phrase, "in the same way" (verse 14), means that

Defining Divine Wealth

the principle of God's people supporting the ministry through tithes and offerings carries into the New Testament.

The logical question then is that if God financially blessed his people for obeying his command to support the ministry under the Old Testament, would he also financially bless his people for obeying the same command under the New Testament? The answer is emphatically yes, borne out by the text of 2 Corinthians 9:

> ⁶ The point is this: whoever sows sparingly will also reap sparingly, and whoever sows bountifully will also reap bountifully.
>
> ⁷ Each one must give as he has decided in his heart, not reluctantly or under compulsion, for God loves a cheerful giver.
>
> ⁸ **And God is able to make all grace abound to you, so that having all sufficiency in all things at all times, you may abound in every good work.**
>
> ¹¹ **You will be enriched in every way to be generous in every way**, which through us will produce thanksgiving to God.
>
> 2 Corinthians 9:6–8, 11 (ESV)

Returning to this text, we see how Paul's teaching is completely consistent with God's pattern of enriching his people financially so their needs can be met and they can be a blessing to others.

To review, let us reiterate the biblical definition of *rich*. Paul defined *rich* in the following ways:

- God causing all grace to abound to you, so in all things, always having all that you need, you will abound in every good work.

- God making you rich in every way so you can be generous all the time.

Therefore, being made rich biblically means to have your own needs met, with plenty left over to generously give to the work of God. This includes supporting the clergy, the local church and assisting the poor.

God's means of using his people in this manner is to financially enrich them, then to call them to willingly give part of their resources to support the Gospel; this is consistent with his dealings with man throughout the ages. God is glorified through this virtuous cycle in which the believer is made rich (that is to say, reaps generously) so he can continue to give generously to the work of God.

In the next chapter, we will look at the difference between divine prosperity and worldly prosperity.

Worldly Prosperity

THERE IS A BIG difference between being rich in the kingdom of Christ and being rich in the world's system. For example, earlier we elaborated on the difference between divine wisdom and worldly, demonic wisdom (see chapter 11). Although both are forms of wisdom, their origin is very significant. The same is true with money. There is a wealth that comes from heaven, and there is a wealth that comes from this world's system.

The world's system refers to Satan's influence on the earth. Because of man's sin and rebellion against God, Satan has been able to establish a kingdom that exerts its influence through wicked governments, false religions, and corrupt financial systems. For example, although God made gold for the benefit of man, lust for gold has been the cause of untold suffering and sin. Human history is rife with accounts of nations destroying or enslaving other nations because they coveted their land and resources.

Satan's prosperity is so apparent that God's people, through the ages, have asked with vexation, "Why do the wicked prosper?" (Psalms 73, Job 21:7ff). Because wealth is a blessing, why are the wicked enjoying it? The answer is that God gave man dominion over the earth and its resources; therefore, man determines how the resources will be used. Because man is enslaved to sin, and, therefore, under the control of Satan, it is no wonder that the wicked prosper. Satan has deceived men into pursuing money instead of God.

Few writers have written as graphically about the worldly system of prosperity than the apostle John. In Revelation, John writes about the world system that he refers to as "Babylon." In Revelation 18, John reveals that the hallmark of this world system is extravagant wealth:

> ² And he shouted with a mighty voice, She is fallen! Mighty Babylon is fallen! She has become a resort and dwelling place for demons, a dungeon haunted by every loathsome spirit, an abode for every filthy and detestable bird.
>
> ³ For all nations have drunk the wine of her passionate unchastity, and the rulers and leaders of the earth have joined with her in committing fornication (idolatry), and **the businessmen of the earth have become rich with the wealth of her excessive luxury and wantonness.**
>
> ⁴ I then heard another voice from heaven saying, **Come out from her, my people, so that you may not share in her sins, neither participate in her plagues.**
>
> Revelation 18:2-4 (Amplified Bible)

"Excessive luxury" and "wantonness" characterize the Babylonian system. In the Babylonian system of finance, there is no restraint, as excess is the order of the day. John condemns this debauchery as idolatry. John is not condemning participation in the world of commerce and trade. He is condemning an evil system that is an unholy copy of God's perfect order. The Babylon system in Revelation describes counterfeit prosperity.

Honest Labor as Opposed to Worldly Prosperity

To clarify, worldly prosperity does not refer to people who work hard at an honest living, save and invest their money, and prosper as a result. Financially successful people are not wicked by default. Work is a godly virtue, and God, in his wisdom, has extended the common grace of work as a means of prosperity to all men, despite their faith in him. The terms *prosperity of the wicked* or *worldly prosperity* refer to the following:

- Those who gained wealth, riches, and influence in an ungodly way.
- Those who have an ungodly attitude toward their wealth.
- Those who use their wealth and influence to practice sin and promote iniquity.

For example, some businesses have accumulated vast finances by lending people money at excessively high interest rates and charging exorbitant late fees. These kinds of businesses target the poor and the financially vulnerable, thus perpetuating a system of debt slavery that borrowers have a difficult time escaping. This is an example of *worldly prosperity*.

There are those who crave money and will do almost anything to get it. Some will sacrifice their relationship with God and their relationship with their family and friends to pursue financial gain. There are people who have made money in legitimate ways, but now use their wealth to pursue a life of sin, and by their actions, they promote an ungodly lifestyle.

Pride and excess motivate the world's system of prosperity, and it works by oppression and deception. The carnal person seeks to prosper so they can flaunt and hoard their wealth, and often their prosperity is at the expense of others (Proverbs 22:16).

The World's System is Not the Church's System

Many Christians do not seem to understand that the world's system of prosperity is not for them. As a result, they are pursuing worldly strategies for prosperity and neglecting to follow God's divine methods of prosperity. Instead of giving with a proper attitude and putting God first through Christian service, many believers follow various schemes to get money. This is why there is so much debt and financial stress in the Church. We have forgotten the wisdom of one of the earth's wisest men:

> [22] The blessing of the LORD makes one rich,
> And He adds no sorrow with it.
>
> Proverbs 10:22 (NKJV)

God's path to financial security may take longer and will be difficult on the flesh nature. Nevertheless, if we follow the

Worldly Prosperity

Bible, we will avoid the heartache and stress that comes from following the Babylonian financial system.

Given the inferiority of worldly prosperity, why do Christians trust in this system so much? For one, many believers attend churches that do not teach about money and finances, and, therefore, they remain ignorant of God's perspective. This ignorance finally leads to financial loss (Hosea 4:6).

Second, worldly prosperity is a system that is based on the senses, and it is easier to walk by sight than by faith. God's people are following the world's system because they have developed faith in what they can see and mentally grasp, instead of developing faith in God's Word (which they cannot see, and must grasp spiritually to operate within it).

Consider this sequence of events: There is *Joe Believer* who sits in his living room, deep in debt, surfing TV channels. As he clicks through the channels, his mind is worrying about his bills. He comes to a religious show featuring a nattily dressed preacher who is delivering a sermon on prosperity. The preacher declares that if Christians give, then it will be given back to them, and, therefore, that believers should take a step of faith and give an offering to the Lord's work. As the preacher preaches and Scriptures flash on the TV screen, Joe Believer becomes indignant.

That man is a fraud! He is just trying to get my money! Whoever heard of God making people rich? The Bible doesn't really say that. This is a cult! In fact, I hear that guy has an airplane and two Mercedes!

He angrily turns to another channel. He comes to an infomercial channel. A handsome, well-dressed man is talking about how anybody can make money by following his prosperity system. As he describes his revolutionary, yet simple, strategy for generating unlimited wealth, a lovely mansion, and two expensive automobiles sit in the background. There is a cut to a shot of him boarding his private jet. Best of all, if you buy his course and apply his methods, you can have what he has: a beautiful, palatial home, a gorgeous spouse, fancy automobiles, and financial freedom. You can be free from the rat race. You will not be chained to a cubicle anymore. You will not have to fight traffic every morning. You can work just a few hours a week from home.

As Joe Believer watches the presentation, the gears of his mind turn excitedly. *Hmm . . . maybe there is something to this. $79.99 is not a lot to spend on his course. Maybe this could be my ticket out of this life of debt that I've been living. In fact, maybe this is God's answer to my prayers!*

The fact is that both systems can produce results. However, the infomercial pitch is appealing to Joe's flesh. The infomercial makes sales by arousing covetous desires that cloud the senses. The man in the infomercial is not telling you everything. He gives you the impression that you can make thousands of dollars a day by working from home in your pajamas for two or three hours a day, but the reality will not be what you think. Eventually, this worldly path to prosperity will bring sorrow, disappointment, and grief to the believer. Joe Believer would have been much better off learning how to employ God's financial system in his life!

Worldly Prosperity

Although the wicked do prosper sometimes, their prosperity is neither lasting nor satisfying (Psalms 74). We should not trust in this world's system because, unlike God's spiritual system that is incorruptible, the world's system is temporal and unreliable. The apostle John warned that the vast riches obtained by this world's system could be brought to naught at a moment's notice:

> [16] Alas, alas for the great city that was robed in fine linen, in purple and scarlet, bedecked and glittering with gold, with precious stones, and with pearls!
>
> [17] **Because in one [single] hour all the vast wealth has been destroyed (wiped out).**
>
> Revelation 18:16–17a (Amplified)

Although John wrote these verses long ago, in modern times we have seen glimpses of how rapidly a national economy can collapse. It is foolish for the believer to trust in this world's financial system, and it is the responsibility of the ministry to teach and guide the Church about God's system of financial blessing.

The Scripture presents two kinds of financial prosperity: wealth that comes from the world's system, driven by greed, and wealth that comes from the kingdom of God—the inheritance of the righteous and received by faith. There is an important distinction between the two, and in the next chapter, we will look at the subject of greed in depth.

Understanding Greed

> [14] Jesus replied, "Man, who appointed me a judge or an arbiter between you?"
>
> [15] Then he said to them, "Watch out! Be on your guard against all kinds of greed; life does not consist in an abundance of possessions."
>
> Luke 12:14-15 (NIV)

GREED IS AN EXTRAORDINARILY destructive evil that can damn a soul. Greed means an excessive desire to acquire things, a preoccupation with material things more than spiritual or intellectual things, and it is characterized by carnal and depraved sensuality. The scriptural prohibition against greed is so strong that the apostles equated greed with idolatry (Colossians 3:5).

A surprising number of people confuse having things or desiring things with being greedy. Wanting things or being rich differs from covetousness. As Jesus taught, greed is not shown by one's possessions, but the corrupt attitude toward those possessions. Often, people crave money so they can fulfill sinful passions and desires. The apostle James wrote:

> ² You desire and you do not have; you murder and envy and you cannot obtain; you quarrel and fight. You do not have because you do not ask;
>
> ³ you ask and do not receive **because you ask wrongly, so you can spend it on your passions.**
>
> James 4:2–3 (NET)

Covetousness or greed can manifest itself in many ways:

- Constantly worrying about money and possessions.
- Pursuing money and riches to the neglect of spiritual and family responsibilities.
- Being envious of other people's possessions and bitter that certain people have what you do not.
- Loving money and possessions more than God.

Clearly, divine financial prosperity and greed for money are two different concepts. Believing God for godly needs and desires differs from lusting for money or craving something that belongs to someone else. Some Christians, unfortunately, conflate the two, and, therefore feel compelled to pursue a life free of material wants and pleasures. Furthermore, religious traditions have implied that to desire something expensive is to be covetous. This is not true.

Throughout human history, God's people have owned and enjoyed exceedingly precious and valuable commodities. God himself likes expensive things. For example, he not only required that

Understanding Greed

the Tabernacle be made of the very finest and most precious of materials, but commanded that Aaron and the priests have special garments made for "glory and for beauty" (Exodus 28:2). Aaron's garments were made with expensive fabric and adorned with gold and rare jewels. God not only wanted his tabernacle and priests to be beautifully adorned, he also wants his people to have good items as well (Psalms 112:1–3). Because God delights in giving his children good things, it follows that his children would delight in receiving them.

Although it is not wrong to desire or have possessions, Christians are strongly warned to protect themselves against the destructive sin of greed. Note Paul's warnings about greed in his letter to Timothy:

> [9] But those who crave to be rich fall into temptation and a snare and into many foolish (useless, godless) and hurtful desires that plunge men into ruin and destruction and miserable perishing.
>
> [10] For the love of money is a root of all evils; it is through this craving that some have been led astray and have wandered from the faith and pierced themselves through with many acute [mental] pangs.
>
> 1 Timothy 6: 9–10 (Amplified)

Because only believers can wander from the faith, Paul is writing about what can happen to Christians who succumb to greed. Craving to be rich and loving money can corrupt the Christian soul to where the believer strays from God, is "plunged into ruin and destruction and miserable perishing," and pierces himself with "many acute [mental] pangs."

Anyone who has suffered great financial loss through unwise decisions that were driven by covetousness can relate to these verses. The severe stress that comes from the regret and humiliation of being plunged into financial distress can completely rob the child of God of their peace and their testimony.

Note again that the apostle Paul is warning against **craving** wealth and **loving** money, not having money or just desiring money. Paul did **not** say, *having money is the root of all evil* or that *those who are rich fall into temptation and a snare.*

Gluttony closely parallels greed and illustrates the difference between an acceptable desire for money and greed. A person may enjoy the food that he or she eats, and look forward to having a delicious meal. However, gluttony is a completely different level of desiring food. It is craving food and eating to excess. It is beyond what is normal, necessary, or temperate. The solution to the sin of gluttony is not abstinence from food. It is discipline. Similarly, the answer to covetousness is not voluntary impoverishment but generous giving (1 Timothy 6:18). It is the responsibility of every believer to understand this distinction and put it into practice in his or her daily life.

We see this distinction between being greedy and proper desire if we compare 1 Timothy 6 with 2 Corinthians 9 in modern translations:

> [11] He will make you rich in every way so that you can always give freely. And your giving through us will cause many to give thanks to God.
>
> 2 Corinthians 9:11 (NCV)

> [9] But those who crave to be rich fall into temptation and a snare and into many foolish (useless, godless) and hurtful desires that plunge men into ruin and destruction and miserable perishing.
>
> 1 Timothy 6: 9 (Amplified)

In 2 Corinthians 9, Paul teaches that God wants the Church to have their needs abundantly met and to generously give to others. It is right, therefore for any Christian to desire money for these reasons. In 1 Timothy 6, however, Paul warns Christians not to **crave** to be rich, especially where the craving is fueled by godless or useless desires. Desiring wealth for godly purposes and craving money for ungodly purposes represent different attitudes.

God is a loving heavenly Father who allows his children a measure of ever-increasing latitude and discretion, as any attentive parent would. For example, when my son was a toddler, my wife and I fed him to make sure that he had the proper food. If we did not watch everything he ate, he was likely to pick food off the ground and eat it, because he did not know any better. Although my son needed that kind of support, I expect my teenage daughter to exercise her own judgment about food. When she goes downtown with her friends, I do not expect her to call me and say, *Should I eat this or that?* I expect that she would have the ability to make those decisions herself.

Similarly, God expects us to make judgments about our own lives and our own needs. If we have a desire, then we have the license to ask the Father and to expect that need to be met. Because it is possible to ask imperfectly (James 4:3); that is, to ask for things that are not good for us or reflect covetous desires, it is the continuing responsibility for every Christian to differentiate between godly and ungodly desires.

It is a mistake to underestimate the seductive power of money and the danger of greed. In the next chapter, we will consider biblical examples of greed.

Portraits of Greed

IN LUKE 12, JESUS told an interesting story about a wealthy man who received an abundant harvest from his crops. He decided to tear down his barns to build bigger ones to store his bounty. He only thought about his own comfort as he planned for a life of relaxation and pleasure. This was a costly miscalculation as God had a different plan:

> [20] But God said to him, 'Fool! This night your soul is required of you, and the things you have prepared, whose will they be?'
> [21] So is the one who lays up treasure for himself and is not rich toward God."
>
> Luke 12: 20-21 (ESV)

This story gives additional insight into greed. The rich man's transgressions, which finally led to his destruction, were not that he had wealth, but that his greed caused him to neglect his spiritual responsibilities to his Creator. When even more prosperity came his way, he had no thought for others, only for himself and his comfortable lifestyle. Not even all his money could settle his sin debt, and because he made no effort to get right with God, he paid dearly for it.

A Conversation Between Two Rich Men

Jesus taught another story that underscores our attitude toward money not money itself that becomes a snare to the soul. Consider the rich man Dives:

> [19] "There was a rich man who was clothed in purple and fine linen and who feasted sumptuously every day.
>
> [20] And at his gate was laid a poor man named Lazarus, covered with sores,
>
> [21] who desired to be fed with what fell from the rich man's table. Moreover, even the dogs came and licked his sores.
>
> [22] The poor man died and was carried by the angels to Abraham's side. The rich man also died and was buried,
>
> [23] and in Hades, being in torment, he lifted up his eyes and saw Abraham far off and Lazarus at his side.
>
> [24] And he called out, 'Father Abraham, have mercy on me, and send Lazarus to dip the end of his finger in water and cool my tongue, for I am in anguish in this flame.'
>
> [25] But Abraham said, 'Child, remember that you in your lifetime received your good things, and Lazarus in like manner bad things; but now he is comforted here, and you are in anguish.
>
> [26] And besides all this, between us and you a great chasm has been fixed, in order that those who would pass from here to you may not be able, and none may cross from there to us.'
>
> Luke 16:19–26 (ESV)

If Abraham was not mentioned in this teaching, one might conclude that it was Dives' wealth that landed him in the place of torment. However, Abraham **is** in this parable, and because

Abraham was very rich (Genesis 13:1), we cannot come to that conclusion. Note that Abraham was a rich man in Paradise, and Dives, a rich man, finished in hell. What was the difference? Obedience: Abraham pursued God and lived a life of faith, while Dives pursued a life of pleasure and hardened his heart to the obvious commands of God to be merciful to those in need. Think how consumed with greed Dives must have been to deny even the scraps from his table to a hungry, suffering soul laid at his doorstep! Dives was condemned because of his disobedient and merciless attitude.

Jesus' parable is an example of two kinds of prosperity at work on the earth: a spiritual prosperity that seeks to please God, and a worldly, carnal prosperity that is motivated by greed and selfish pleasure.

As we consider these passages, we can see how ignorance and religious tradition has corrupted our understanding of what Jesus said. The Church has had the idea that our heavenly Father is against us having money or wealth, and that to be rich is to be worldly. We read Scriptures about rich people going to hell and we think, *It's better not to be rich.* This presents a grave dilemma for the Church, because we need money to meet our own needs and to pay for ministry endeavors. However, based on Christ's own words, having material things is not the issue. Jesus is concerned about us **becoming covetous** and **worrying** whether our needs will be met. Our attitude should be to have faith; we set our hearts not on obtaining things, but on seeking the kingdom of God and his righteousness.

Importantly, it is crucial for believers to differentiate between wanting and having finances and being greedy. Following are two incidents in the Old Testament that illustrate the difference.

Achan and the Misery of Greed

Achan was an Israelite soldier serving under Joshua when the children of Israel began to take possession of the Promised Land. Scripture immortalizes him as the man who coveted and took precious things during the fall of Jericho. His greed cost him and his family their lives (Joshua 7).

Achan was just a child when Caleb, the leader of his tribe, went with eleven other spies to investigate the land of Canaan. After an extensive sojourn, the spies came back and confirmed Canaan's rich abundance. However, ten of the spies also stated that there were giants living there and that the land was one that "devoured its inhabitants." Israel believed this negative report and refused to trust God to enter into the Promised Land. For that mistake, God punished Israel by preventing them from entering the land, and that generation of adults who refused to trust God perished in the wilderness (Numbers 14:30–35).

The generation of Achan grew to adulthood, wandering for forty years in the desert. Because Caleb did not perish with the other spies because he believed God, Achan probably heard Caleb recount the incident many times. Perhaps more than any other generation of Israelites, Achan's generation understood, within their core, that the Word of God must be obeyed to the uttermost. This is why the Israelites agreed to fully follow

Joshua, and to disobey his commands would mean death to the transgressor (Joshua 1:17–18).

God gave Moses and Joshua very specific instructions about the conquest of Canaan (Deuteronomy 7:16–26). Although sometimes, Israel was allowed to keep some plunder for themselves, certain cities were totally given over to destruction; that is, every living thing had to be killed and all the bounty had to be given to God's treasury. Furthermore, God warned that if any Israelite took any plunder from these banned cities for themselves, they would become cursed and would be set apart for destruction. Jericho was one of these cities, and Joshua made this clear to his army:

> [17] The city and all that is in it must be set apart for the Lord, except for Rahab the prostitute and all who are with her in her house, because she hid the spies we sent.
>
> [18] But be careful when you are setting apart the riches for the Lord. If you take any of it, you will make the Israelite camp subject to annihilation and cause a disaster.
>
> [19] All the silver and gold, as well as bronze and iron items, belong to the Lord. They must go into the Lord's treasury."
>
> Joshua 6:17–19 (NET)

This background is essential to understanding the enormity of Achan's sin. Achan desired the material things of this world more than he desired to keep God's explicit and oft-repeated commands. It was not just that Achan desired something impressive; he willfully rebelled against God's clear purpose. The result was not only Israel being defeated in battle before the men of Ai, but Achan himself was found out, and he and his family were killed in a terrifying manner:

> ²⁴ And Joshua and all Israel with him took Achan the son of Zerah, and the silver and the cloak and the bar of gold, and his sons and daughters and his oxen and donkeys and sheep and his tent and all that he had. And they brought them up to the Valley of Achor.
>
> ²⁵ And Joshua said, "Why did you bring trouble on us? The LORD brings trouble on you today." And all Israel stoned him with stones. They burned them with fire and stoned them with stones.
>
> ²⁶ And they raised over him a great heap of stones that remains to this day. Then the LORD turned from his burning anger. Therefore, to this day the name of that place is called the Valley of Achor.
>
> Joshua 7:24–26 (ESV)

Ironically, in their next conquest, God allowed the Israelites to keep the plunder of their victory:

> ¹ And the LORD said to Joshua, "Do not fear and do not be dismayed. Take all the fighting men with you, and arise, go up to Ai. See, I have given into your hand the king of Ai, and his people, his city, and his land.
>
> ² And you shall do to Ai and its king as you did to Jericho and its king. Only its spoil and its livestock you shall take as plunder for yourselves. Lay an ambush against the city, behind it."
>
> Joshua 8:1–2 (ESV)

God had no problem transferring the wealth and lands of Canaan to Israel, both collectively and individually, but he also required strict obedience from his people. Certainly, whatever Achan would have been willing to give up for the Lord in Jericho, he would have gotten back in the conquest of Ai and the other cities. Unfortunately, he never lived to see that fulfilled.

The Intemperance of Gehazi

Elisha was a powerful prophet in Israel who had an attendant named Gehazi. In those days, it was common for prophets to have men who would serve under them in ministry (for example, Elisha served under Elijah).

Elisha performed wondrous miracles in the name of the Lord, and Gehazi became a witness to miracles that few men have ever seen. He saw, up close, the strength of Elisha's ministry and the depth of his character. However, greed would be Gehazi's undoing.

The book of 2 Kings records a story where a famous Syrian general named Naaman came to Elisha to be healed of leprosy (2 Kings 5). Elisha did not even go out to meet Naaman, but unceremoniously instructed him through a messenger to wash seven times in the Jordan River. Naaman was angry that Elisha did not do something more dramatic and dignified and he considered leaving. However, one of Naaman's slaves urged him to do what Elisha instructed, and after doing so, Naaman was completely healed of leprosy. Out of gratitude, Naaman offered Elisha expensive gifts, which Elisha steadfastly refused. After parting words, Naaman went back to his own land.

Having seen the fine gifts that Naaman had offered, Gehazi decided that Elisha had missed out by letting Naaman go without receiving his gift. Therefore, Gehazi ran after Naaman, and concocted a story that Elisha had sent him to receive money and clothing for some guest prophets who had just arrived from a far country. Naaman happily obliged and gave Gehazi silver and two sets of clothing. Unfortunately for Gehazi, Elisha found out what had happened and pronounced a curse on him for his avarice and deceit:

> [25] When he came and stood before his master, Elisha asked him, "Where have you been, Gehazi?" He answered, "Your servant hasn't been anywhere."
>
> [26] Elisha replied, "I was there in spirit when a man turned and got down from his chariot to meet you. This is not the proper time to accept silver or to accept clothes, olive groves, vineyards, sheep, cattle, and male and female servants.
>
> [27] Therefore Naaman's skin disease will afflict you and your descendants forever!" When Gehazi went out from his presence, his skin was as white as snow.
>
> 2 Kings 5:25–27 (NET)

Elisha told Gehazi that it was not the proper time to accept material things because Elisha did not want God's glory diminished. Naaman was not an Israelite, and was sent to Israel by the king of Syria. God healed this famous general to bring glory to himself among the Gentiles. Imagine the witness and testimony when Naaman, a former leper, returned to his country healed! If Elisha had accepted a monetary gift from Naaman, it would have diminished the grace of God by suggesting that

God's gift of healing had to be bought. Gehazi's greed blinded him to the spiritual significance of this miracle. The penalty that Gehazi had to endure was the leprosy of Naaman, not only on himself, but also on his descendants. The stories of Achan and Gehazi illuminate the importance of limits and discretion.

The Prosperity of Our Portion

From the tragic story of Achan, we learn that although God wants his people to be rich and abundantly supplied, there are some things that God's people cannot have. God has set boundaries to the believer's prosperity, and these boundaries are for our own good. Ancient Israel frequently called God's physical boundaries and limits a *portion* or a *lot* or *allotment*. This concept of limits is found throughout Scripture:

- Although God gave Israel an exceedingly prosperous and abundant land in Canaan, he strictly warned Moses not to seek to take possession of the lands of Moab and Edom, because their lands were not given to them.

- Israel was required by God to give the first fruits of all their increase, the tithe, and to bring it to the place of worship. Withholding the tithe was a boundary that Israel was not to violate.

- Each of the twelve tribes was given a specific allotment of the land of Canaan. However, the Levites were not given a land-based inheritance because the ministry was their portion.

- God required Israel not to harvest to the borders of their farms, so the poor could glean the leftovers, and thereby, have food to eat.

- The tenth commandment that God wrote with his own finger is, "Thou shall not covet." Desiring what belongs to another person, whether it is a spouse, a servant or a material possession, was extremely wicked in God's sight, and represented a clear boundary that should not be crossed.

Understanding the concept of limits and portion will allow us to sidestep the pitfalls that many Christians fall into when believing God for prosperity. Although, conceptually, it is not out of bounds for a Christian to desire and ask God for a house on a hill, it is prudent to stop and pray, *Lord, is this desire right for me now? Is it consistent with the portion that you have provided for me now?* Although God loves all his children equally, and each child of God is equally qualified to receive his or her inheritance, the Scriptures do not teach that every child of God gets the same portion. Some will get more than others will (Matthew 25:14–30). The promise of divine financial prosperity is given in context to our relationship with God. As we trust God, the Holy Spirit will help us to understand when, how and what to receive.

In his book, *Faith Dynamics*, Dr. Ken Chant gives insight into exercising faith within boundaries:

> *No one in fact, can exercise faith at all, in a Christian setting, beyond what God has determined for his or her life. This must be so; for Christian faith has such limitless possibilities, as big as God himself, that it must be confined to the limits of God's will for each person. Our responsibility, under the direction of the Holy Spirit, is to discover the things that require faith from each one of us personally, and then to set ourselves to believe for those things, and no others. To try to exercise faith for anything that lies outside of God's purpose is to step from faith into presumption – which is a certain way to ruin.*[15]

Although there are practical limits to the human exercise of faith, the concept of portion is consistent with the biblical truths of abundance and overflow. David said, "**My** cup runneth over." He also wrote that the "boundary lines have fallen **for me** in delightsome places." A cup represents a specified amount, and although the size of our cup may be smaller than others, God wants to fill it to overflowing so we will be abundantly satisfied. Thus, my portion will still be more than enough for me. Paul speaks of this type of provision:

---

[15] As it is written, "Whoever gathered much had nothing left over, and whoever gathered little had no lack."

2 Corinthians 8:15 (ESV)

The key to walking in divine prosperity is to understand your portion, or place in God. Be at peace with what the Lord shows you, and then it will be easier to receive prosperity from the Lord. This ties to what Jesus said, "Seek ye first the kingdom of God and all these things will be added to you."

The kingdom of God is purely God's rule and reign in our lives. When we seek first God's rule in our lives, including the boundaries he has set, then the things we need and desire will come to us.

The Prosperity of Restraint

From Gehazi, we learn that there are times when the Lord calls us to set aside our desire for things and exercise restraint for the greater good of his kingdom. Although Elisha was entitled to a prophet's reward, he had enough judgment to understand that refraining under the circumstances would increase God's glory. As Christians, we must realize that there are times in our lives when we are called to restrain ourselves from receiving what might be considered "our due." Some examples:

- A gifted medical student may, for a season, provide services among the poor and needy, though she could rightfully earn a much higher compensation in a prestigious and wealthy practice.
- Missionaries may serve in countries where the comforts of their homeland may not exist.

- Ministers may be called to a ministry opportunity where they serve without pay, though they are entitled to a salary.

Putting into practice the biblical disciplines of limits, restraint, and temperance will position us to continually receive God's best for our lives.

Biblical Ways to Overcome Greed

HAVING EXPLORED THE DANGERS of greed, we turn our attention to some insights into overcoming greed. They are:

- Not being haughty
- Giving
- Being content

Do Not Be Haughty

> [17] As for the rich in this present age, charge them not to be haughty, nor to set their hopes on the uncertainty of riches, but on God, who richly provides us with everything to enjoy.
>
> [18] They are to do good, to be rich in good works, to be generous and ready to share,
>
> [19] thus storing up treasure for themselves as a good foundation for the future, so that they may take hold of that which is truly life.
>
> 1 Timothy 6:17–19 (ESV)

In this passage, Paul provides the answer to the extremely serious problem of greed. The first part of the answer has to do with attitude. Do not be arrogant or put your hope in money. Craving wealth comes about when people begin to intensely focus on money and what it can do and what it provides. They begin to see money as the primary source of the things they need and want. If they actually get the money, then they become haughty and lifted up in pride; they believe they have no need of anything. Therefore, greed is having a perverse faith in money. Paul presents the correct attitude when he writes that the rich should put their trust in God: "who richly provides us with everything to enjoy." Faith in money leads to greed, which ultimately leads to destruction, misery, and mental torment. Faith in God leads to the same material abundance, without the suffering and sorrow that accompany covetousness (Proverbs 10:22).

Give

The second part of the answer has to do with action. The rich are to "do good, be rich in good deeds, to be generous and ready to share." If money itself were the problem, then the apostle would have simply told Timothy to command the rich to give away their possessions. Instead, Paul commands the rich to become committed to good works and act generously. This is entirely consistent with Paul's teaching on the purpose of divine wealth in 2 Corinthians:

> ⁷ Each one must give as he has decided in his heart, not reluctantly or under compulsion, for God loves a cheerful giver.
>
> ⁸ And God is able to make all grace abound to you, so that having all sufficiency in all things at all times, **you may abound in every good work.**
>
> 2 Corinthians 9:7–8 (ESV)

God wants to make us rich, not as an end in itself, but so that our needs will be met and we will then be able to perform good works and continue to be generous to those in need. When wealthy people sincerely and earnestly devote themselves to helping others and generously sharing their riches, they are proving that they are not covetous.

Be Content

Contentment is also a solution to greed.

> ⁵ Keep your life free from love of money, and **be content** with what you have, for he has said, "I will never leave you nor forsake you."
>
> ⁶ So we can confidently say,
> "The Lord is my helper;
> I will not fear;
> what can man do to me?"
>
> Hebrews 13:5–6 (ESV)

For present-day Americans, the word *content* probably has a different shade of meaning from what Paul intended. The translated Greek word means *to be sufficient, to be possessed of suffi-*

cient strength, to be strong, to be enough. It also carries the meaning, *to defend, or ward off.*[16] It is this Greek word that is used in these scriptures:

> [11] Not that I am speaking of being in need, for I have learned in whatever situation I am to be **content**.
>
> Philippians 4:11 (ESV)

> [6] But godliness with **contentment** is great gain,
>
> I Timothy 6:6 (ESV)

> [8] And God is able to make all grace abound to you, so that having all **sufficiency** in all things at all times, you may abound in every good work.
>
> 2 Corinthians 9:8 (ESV)

In this context, contentment does not mean passively accepting life's circumstances, but rather having the things we need. This sufficiency is based on our relationship with Christ, and rests on God's promises to help us and meet our needs. Therefore, our contentment in Christ is a sure defense against both lack and the love of money.

To be content is also to understand that we will face trials, adversity, and setbacks that may include financial lack and hardships. These sufferings are real, and often fiery, and are explained more fully in the section on suffering (see part 6). However, suffering is temporary and subject to change, precisely because the Lord is our helper and he will not fail us.

Worldly prosperity is a system that is based on covetousness and the flesh. When we begin to crave the things of this world and love money, we move away from God's plan of prosperity and start to trade in the world's system of wealth. This is a counterfeit system that can only end in ruin and destruction.

Every Christian is called, therefore, to eschew covetousness and to pursue godliness, good works, and generosity. In the next section, we will look at how suffering and prosperity relate.

PART 6
PROSPERITY AND SUFFERING

The Mystery of Suffering

I DO NOT PRESUME to understand the mystery of suffering in the life of the believer. The most erudite explanations of why Christians suffer leave us feeling dissatisfied and yearning for deeper answers. When we consider the mystery of suffering in the light of God's glory, we end up like Job:

> ³ Surely I spoke of things I did not understand, things too wonderful for me to know.
>
> Job 42:3b (NIV).

Job certainly experienced suffering as much as any man, yet, after he engaged with Almighty God, he had to admit that he could not rightly comprehend his trials. Can any of us feel any differently? In addition, despite the teachings of Scripture, we are left to conclude that the judgment of God is ultimately alien to our human understanding–it is God's **strange** work (Isaiah 28:21). Even so, it is essential to relate divine prosperity to the doctrine of suffering for two reasons.

First, as I have said before, divine prosperity is not a stand-alone doctrine that is believed and practiced in isolation to other truths of the Christian faith. An authentic message of prosperity would not contradict or disregard other biblical doctrines such as holiness, evangelism, patience, or suffering. The persistent criticism of the "prosperity message" is that this line of teaching refutes Christian suffering. In this chapter, I will show that this is not true.

Second, the better the understanding that a believer has of suffering, the better they will be able to understand why they are not prospering or why their prosperity may be delayed. For example, financial trials could represent God's chastisement, and the believer should respond to those circumstances differently from those of financial adversity instigated by Satan. Believers are better able to walk in victory when they are able to understand the source and reason of suffering in their lives.

Suffering and divine prosperity are not incompatible, opposite conditions. Although both are biblical truths, they are distinct and operate in very different ways. Besides this, there are various types of suffering.

I use the word *suffering* in an extremely broad sense. It may refer to any of the trials, persecutions, hard places, obstacles, disappointments, and tragedies that Christians may face in their lives. The word *suffering* also captures the spiritual and emotional distress caused by these adverse circumstances. For example, the darkness of financial problems is more oppressive because of the emotional torment that comes from being deeply in debt and facing severe financial shortages.

The Mystery of Suffering

The apostle Peter wrote extensively about suffering in his first epistle, clearly explaining that there were different types of suffering:

> [12] Beloved, do not be surprised at the fiery trial when it comes upon you to test you, as though something strange were happening to you.
>
> [13] But rejoice insofar as you share Christ's sufferings, that you may also rejoice and be glad when his glory is revealed.
>
> [14] If you are insulted for the name of Christ, you are blessed, because the Spirit of glory and of God rests upon you.
>
> [15] But let none of you suffer as a murderer or a thief or an evildoer or as a meddler.
>
> [16] Yet if anyone suffers as a Christian, let him not be ashamed, but let him glorify God in that name.
>
> 1 Peter 4:12–16 (ESV).

> [17] For it is better to suffer for doing good, if that should be God's will, than for doing evil.
>
> 1 Peter 3:17 (ESV).

> [19] For this is a gracious thing, when, mindful of God, one endures sorrows while suffering unjustly.
>
> [20] For what credit is it if, when you sin and are beaten for it, you endure? But if when you do good and suffer for it you endure, this is a gracious thing in the sight of God.
>
> [21] For to this you have been called, because Christ also suffered for you, leaving you an example, so that you might follow in his steps.
>
> 1 Peter 2:19–21 (ESV).

The three types of suffering that Peter writes about are:

- Suffering endured as the result of sin (namely, God's judgment).
- Suffering for righteousness' sake.
- The suffering of Christ on behalf of the believer.

Although the above list does not offer a comprehensive guide to the subject of suffering, it serves as a useful baseline for understanding why suffering occurs and how Christians should respond to it. Importantly, Peter's teaching underscores why Christians should not view suffering through a solitary lens. When believers group all forms of suffering into one category, they incorrectly interpret negative circumstances in life. For example, there are Christians who hold God responsible for typical problems: *I got a flat tire this morning and was late for work. I guess the Lord is trying to teach me to slow down a bit.* On the other hand, there are many blaming Satan for all life's problems: *My refrigerator broke down on Saturday, and the milk spoiled. Satan sure is busy!* Alternatively, there are also those who always attribute trials to past mistakes and sins: *My doctor told me I have cancer. I guess the Lord is paying me back for my life of sin when I was younger.*

If we understand suffering through the perspective of only one type of cause, we will not be able to effectively deal with suffering properly.

Suffering for Sin

> ¹⁵ But let none of you suffer as a murderer, or as a thief, or as an evildoer, or as a busybody in other men's matters.
>
> 1 Peter 4:15 (KJV).

PETER TALKED ABOUT SUFFERING because of doing evil, which in essence is suffering because of God's judgment or sin.

God's judgment is progressive and multifaceted, and it is always instigated as a response to human sin and iniquity. The judgment of God is a serious matter that we should not carelessly ascribe to life's circumstances. We should not misrepresent God by interpreting all suffering and tragedies that afflict a person because of divine judgment for some heinous sin. The Bible says that God is slow to anger and does not willingly afflict people (Lamentations 3:33). Jesus Christ bore the wrath of God on the cross, so we would not have to bear it (Romans 5:8–10). Moreover, if the believer sins, then God has made a provision where the child of God can receive forgiveness and cleansing from sin (1 John 1:9). If the erring believer is willing to judge himself and repent of their sins, then he will not be judged (1 Corinthians 11:30–32).

Therefore, as we broach the subject of God's judgment, I emphasize that God does not delight in bringing negative judgment and punishment upon his Church. The Father's plan is that his children receive the Word and act on it, and rely on his grace and forgiveness to go from faith to faith. Even so, God will judge sinners and saints alike if they pursue wickedness and iniquity. Many Scriptures articulate this position, but none so dramatically as Deuteronomy 28. Moses, under the inspiration of the Holy Spirit, boldly declared in minute detail the astounding destruction that God would send upon **his own people** for impenitently disobeying Him.

God's abhorrence of sin and rebellion is not softened in the New Testament. The apostles warned the Church that God would visit his wrath upon believers who refuse to obey him (Matthew 18:33–35, Romans 13:3–5, Ephesians 5:5–7, Hebrews 13:4, 1 Corinthians 10:1–12). Although the judgment of God rightly invokes a reverential fear in the heart of the believer, we are never separated from the grace and goodness of God. For example, consider the Lord's actions on the Corinthians. The apostle Paul explained why divine judgment had come upon some Corinthians:

> [29] For anyone who eats and drinks without discerning the body eats and drinks judgment on himself.
>
> [30] That is why many of you are weak and ill, and some have died.
>
> 1 Corinthians 11:29–30 (ESV).

Suffering for Sin

The Corinthian Christians were partaking of the Lord's Table in an unworthy and irreverent manner, and that, with the other sins, provoked divine discipline. The result was that some became weak and sick and others died. Note that God did not start with the highest form of discipline. He admonished the erring saints through the ministry. When the people would not listen to the ministry, he allowed their physical bodies to become weak and sick, and when they still would not repent, they died prematurely. However, this kind of systematic judgment could have been avoided if the erring saints had judged themselves and repented. Indeed, Paul gives the Corinthian church a principle of God's mercy:

> [31] But if we judged ourselves truly, we would not be judged.
> [32] But when we are judged by the Lord, we are disciplined so that we may not be condemned along with the world.
>
> 1 Corinthians 11:31–32 (ESV).

God will judge sin, but he wants his people to judge themselves and repent. This principle is powerfully illustrated through the words of prophet Amos:

> [6] "I gave you cleanness of teeth in all your cities, and lack of bread in all your places, yet you did not return to me," declares the LORD.
>
> [9] "I struck you with blight and mildew; your many gardens and your vineyards, your fig trees and your olive trees the locust devoured; yet you did not return to me," declares the LORD.
>
> [10] "I sent among you a pestilence after the manner of Egypt; I killed your young men with the sword, and carried away

> your horses, and I made the stench of your camp go up into your nostrils; yet you did not return to me," declares the LORD.
>
> ¹¹ "I overthrew some of you, as when God overthrew Sodom and Gomorrah, and you were as a brand plucked out of the burning; yet you did not return to me," declares the LORD.
>
> ¹² "Therefore thus I will do to you, O Israel; because I will do this to you, prepare to meet your God, O Israel!"
>
> Amos 4:6, 9–12 (NET).

Note how many times the Lord uses the phrase, "yet you did not return to me." God will bring suffering into a believer's life, but the purpose of divine discipline is to bring repentance, restoration, and wholeness. If a believer is going through financial adversity, she should have the courage to examine her own life. She should ask, *Is there sin or disobedience that is causing Father God to withhold his material blessings and bring judgment in my life?* David expressed it this way:

> ²³ Search me, O God, and know my heart: try me, and know my thoughts:
>
> ²⁴ And see if there be any wicked way in me, and lead me in the way everlasting.
>
> Psalms 139:23–24 (KJV).

If we have repented of our sins before our loving and holy Father, he will forgive us and restore us. Then we will have repositioned ourselves to receive God's prosperity in our lives.

Although it is not pleasant to talk about God's wrath and judgment, we must allow it to become part of our theological framework. If we accept the Word of God on divine financial prosperity, then we must also accept that those glorious promises are forfeited if we pursue a life of sin and rebellion.

Suffering as a Consequence of Our Sins

One form of God's judgment is to suffer the consequences of our sins. We all sin; suffering the consequences of sin is one aspect of divine judgment. Although God forgives us of our sins (1 John 1:9), we have to deal with the consequences of our actions and these consequences often manifest themselves as tribulations. For example, many Christians have financial problems because they repeatedly make poor financial decisions. They save too little, borrow too much, and spend, spend, spend.

The Scriptures also point to a less commonly cited reason that God's people suffer financially: laziness. Throughout Scripture, God's people are commanded to work diligently. The Bible explicitly commends education, apprenticeship, artisanship, faithfulness, and integrity in the realm of work and exalts all honest labor. Even so, some Christians get the idea that they do not have to work, and that serving God means living off the charity of other people. The apostle Paul, in particular, addressed this error head on and sternly warned the Church:

> [10] For even when we were with you, we would give you this command: If anyone is not willing to work, let him not eat.
>
> 2 Thessalonians 3:10 (ESV).

Note this is a commandment and rule for Christian living as much as the principle as giving and receiving. The meaning here is clear: if you are a lazy Christian, then you will not prosper. You will constantly experience financial trials and the cause of these is your disobedience.

Christians often experience financial heartaches when they take to heart the world's attitudes toward money. Worldly prosperity systems emphasize *financial freedom*. The goal of worldly prosperity is to have so much money that you can do whatever you want, when you want. This concept is totally at odds with divine prosperity. Divine prosperity is financial empowerment so the believer can be a better servant of God. However, as the apostle Paul warned, some men, seeking to be rich, have followed wrong and hurtful ways and pierced themselves with many griefs.

Suffering Because of God's Chastisement

Chastisement refers to how God perfects his people through discipline, hardship, and affliction, and it is not always the result of specific sins. Chastisement and judgment are very closely related concepts, but they are different. Paralleling Jesus' teaching about the gardener pruning a vine (John 15), chastisement involves God lovingly cutting away the things in a believer's life that are displeasing to him, without harming the actual person. In this sense, the suffering that comes because of being chastised does not fit neatly in Peter's category of suffering as an evildoer, or suffering because of righteousness. Even so, I classify chastisement in the category of judgment, because often, God chastises the Church because we have a tendency to go astray and need chastisement to be brought back on track.

For example, the writer of Hebrews referred to the suffering of the Hebrew Christians as spiritual discipline designed for their good:

> ⁵ And have you forgotten the exhortation that addresses you as sons? "My son, do not regard lightly the discipline of the Lord,
> nor be weary when reproved by him.
> ⁶ **For the Lord disciplines the one he loves, and chastises every son whom he receives."**
>
> Hebrews 12:5–6 (ESV).

> ⁹ Besides this, we have had earthly fathers who disciplined us and we respected them. Shall we not much more be subject to the Father of spirits and live?
> ¹⁰ For they disciplined us for a short time as it seemed best to them, but he disciplines us for our good, that we may share his holiness.
> ¹¹ **For the moment all discipline seems painful rather than pleasant, but later it yields the peaceful fruit of righteousness to those who have been trained by it.**
>
> Hebrews 12:9–11 (ESV).

These passages explain that God used painful adversity to counter the Hebrew Christians' stray into apostasy. Although the

Lord has **many** tools that he employs to instruct his people, chastisement is a tool believers conveniently forget. Believers delighted with the prosperity message would do well to remember that the Lord has used **financial adversity** to get his people's attention:

> [7] "Thus says the LORD of hosts: Consider your ways.
>
> [8] Go up to the hills and bring wood and build the house, that I may take pleasure in it and that I may be glorified, says the LORD.
>
> [9] You looked for much, and behold, it came to little. And when you brought it home, I blew it away. Why? declares the LORD of hosts. Because of my house that lies in ruins, while each of you busies himself with his own house.
>
> [10] Therefore the heavens above you have withheld the dew, and the earth has withheld its produce.
>
> [11] And I have called for a drought on the land and the hills, on the grain, the new wine, the oil, on what the ground brings forth, on man and beast, and on all their labors."
>
> Haggai 1:7-11 (ESV).

When we consider passages like Deuteronomy 28, Amos 4, and Haggai 1, and read them naturally, clearly God uses adversity and hardships (financial and otherwise) to goad his people into obedience.

FOR A SEASON AND FOR OUR OWN GOOD

God brings chastisement for a season for our own good. However, that season has a beginning, middle, and an end. The Scripture says that after we have been trained by suffering, such suffering will yield the peaceable fruit of righteousness

(Hebrews 12:11). In Galatians, Paul wrote that Israel was put under the tight supervision of the Law, with its harsh decrees and penalties, the same way that Greek children were made subject to guardians and trustees. God used the severity of the Law to prepare Israel for the coming of Christ.

Some in the Church are suffering financial afflictions as part of God's chastisement. There were some of us who would not respond to his Word, or listen to his preachers, who called the Church to repent of fiscal mismanagement, therefore, God put us under the governance of affliction. As believers, we have had to deal with unscrupulous credit collectors, devious lenders, experience the frustration of seeing most of our earnings go to pay bills, and endure the stress of shortage. However, God intends this only to be for a season. If we repent and align ourselves with his divine plan for prosperity, then God's chastisement will have produced good fruit.

Suffering Because the World is Fallen

SUFFERING ALSO COMES BECAUSE the world is fallen. Obviously, the world is fallen because of God's judgment on Adam's transgression. The consequence of Adam's transgression is that his descendants must live in a world marred by violence, poverty, sickness, and death. Obedience to God, to an extent, shielded his people from the curses that were on the earth. For example, Abraham and his godly line repeatedly experienced supernatural protection. God promised to deliver the nation of Israel from the ravaging effects of sin, sickness, famine, and defeat in war if the people of Israel obeyed the Law (Deuteronomy 28). However, God's people endure various maladies and problems, despite God's promises of protection. Problems persist because the world is fallen. The Fall helps us to understand that there are not perfect correlations between what people do and what happens to them. Sometimes bad things happen to people because the world is dangerous and unpredictable, not because of any good or evil done by the victim. The apostle James reminded the Church that mortal men do not know "what tomorrow will bring" and, therefore, we should not arrogantly presume uninterrupted success (James 4:14). Jesus taught that his followers would have to contend with evil on a daily basis (Matthew 6:34).

The fallen state of the world has a direct impact on our finances. Jesus told his followers not to lay up treasures on the earth where "moth and rust corrupt, and thieves break in and steal" (Matthew 6:19). Here Jesus is explaining that because the world is fallen, and our money is in the world, our wealth is vulnerable: it can be destroyed and it can be stolen.

In 2007, the US began to experience a deep recession predominantly caused because of a massive failure of mortgage-backed securities. The failure of sub-prime mortgages rippled throughout our financial system, freezing credit lines, causing companies to fail, and creating widespread unemployment. The country suffered tremendous destruction of wealth as people drained their life savings trying to save their homes and keep themselves financially afloat. Many journalists have linked the initial problems to the financial chicanery of greedy executives who misrepresented their financial products and services.

Not surprisingly, many Christians and Christian organizations were adversely affected during this downturn. Although they themselves may not have been involved in any kind of fraud, they were affected by the sins of others. This is a classic example of the fleetingness of wealth that Jesus described. Fortunately, Scripture provides the believer with a solution to this dilemma. Although the world is evil and unpredictable, and our wealth can be lost, we are not to put our trust in our money, but in

Suffering Because the World is Fallen

God, who gives us all things for us to richly enjoy (1 Timothy 6:17). When we trust God to be our source, even when we lose our money, he can restore it to us.

Suffering Because of Delays

SPIRITUAL DELAYS ARE A form of suffering. In fact, **all of creation** is in a state of waiting for the sons of God to be revealed and the fullness of redemption (Romans 8:19). The Church is not exempt from having to endure delay. The apostle John wrote in Revelation that the saints cry out before God, "How long?" (Revelation 6:10).

Possibly one of the most difficult aspects of believing God for prosperity in our own lives is that we have to wait with faith and patience for it to manifest. All parents know how trying it can be to instruct children to wait for anything they want. They want to go to McDonald's, but they have to wait. They want to go outside and play, but they have to wait. They want a new toy, but they have to wait. They fidget, they whine, they make faces, and they nag until they can get what they want. Part of the way children become mature is by learning how to wait patiently for the things they want, without whining and complaining. They go about their business doing what they need to do and learn how to wait for the fullness of time to receive their desires. Developing patience in a child is a long and difficult process, but the effort is necessary. In a similar manner, as Christians, we will have to learn how to endure delays in every expression of our faith, including finances.

God establishes things spiritually before they manifest themselves materially. For example, God spoke about the coming Messiah thousands of years before he came. Indeed, God's plan of redemption was completed before the world was created (1 Peter 1:20, Revelation. 13:8), but Christ appeared only at the right time in history (Galatians 4:4). Another example is how God told Abraham that he would be the ancestor of kings and the father of a multitude while he and Sarah were still barren. These examples show that God's timetable is often different from ours.

Nonetheless, God is not the author of all delays. The Bible teaches that evil principalities and powers seek to obstruct heavenly blessings and divine answers to prayer. Daniel described how demonic forces hindered the angel Gabriel in responding to Daniel's prayer:

> [12] Then he said to me, "Fear not, Daniel, for from the first day that you set your heart to understand and humbled yourself before your God, your words have been heard, and I have come because of your words.
>
> [13] **The prince of the kingdom of Persia withstood me twenty-one days**, but Michael, one of the chief princes, came to help me, for I was left there with the kings of Persia,
>
> [14] and came to make you understand what is to happen to your people in the latter days. For the vision is for days yet to come."
>
> Daniel 10:12-14 (ESV).

God sent an angelic answer from the first day Daniel prayed, but it took twenty-one days for the angel to reach Daniel because of demonic interference (the prince of Persia referred to in this passage is an evil principality). This pattern of delay because of the devil is seen in the New Testament. For example, Satan repeatedly hindered Paul from visiting and ministering to the churches of Thessalonica (1 Thessalonians 2:18). The Apostles warned the Church to be on their guard against Satan who fights against believers (Ephesians 6:12, 1 Peter 5:8).

Despite the reasons for the delay occurring, God has given all his children an inheritance. However, this inheritance is received because of faith and patience (Romans 4:13–16, Hebrews 6:12). To have faith is to joyfully expect that the object of our faith is ours and will become apparent before we actually see it. To have patience is to keep steady in faith, believing that we will receive, though the object of our faith is delayed. We are going to have to endure stubborn obstacles, heartbreaking problems, perplexities, and concerns that will shake us to the core, but these are an essential aspect of the Christian life.

While writing from a prison cell Paul taught us "my God shall supply all your needs according to his riches and glory in Christ Jesus" (Philippians 4:19). Here Paul is referring to the *should state* of the giving believer. He is exhorting us that this is where we are headed. We may be locked up; we may be bound with insecurity, debt, and problems. However, if we patiently believe God, we will possess our inheritance and have every need abundantly met.

Suffering for the Sake of Righteousness

> [10] "Blessed are those who are persecuted for righteousness' sake, for theirs is the kingdom of heaven.
>
> [11] "Blessed are you when others revile you and persecute you and utter all kinds of evil against you falsely on my account.
>
> [12] Rejoice and be glad, for your reward is great in heaven, for so they persecuted the prophets who were before you.
>
> Matthew 5:10–12 (ESV).

> [14] But even if you should suffer for righteousness' sake, you are blessed. "And do not be afraid of their threats, nor be troubled."
>
> 1 Peter 3:14 (NKJV).

PETER ALSO TAUGHT THAT there is suffering for the sake of righteousness, or suffering because of doing good and being obedient to the Word of God. In this chapter, I consider whether suffering for the sake of righteousness contradicts our assertion that God wants his people to prosper spiritually, physically, and financially.

A Multifaceted Concept

Suffering for the sake of righteousness is a multifaceted concept. Believers may suffer in many ways for the sake of good. For example, as Peter notes, a servant that is earnestly and respectfully serving his or her master, or employer, may suffer the indignity of harsh treatment and beatings despite his or her exemplary behavior. Believers, who live a quiet life and make it a point not to meddle in the affairs of others, may find themselves maligned and scorned as gossips and busybodies.

Righteous suffering may be internal and silent. Lot was grieved in his heart when he saw the iniquity of his neighbors in Sodom. Jeremiah wept when he witnessed how Israel's sin had devastated the nation. Jesus wept over the unbelief of his people.

Finally, all suffering, including suffering for the sake of righteousness, is temporary. All suffering for the believer ends with death, but even in this life, God has made it that suffering is limited and temporary. Job suffered more than most men, but the blessings that God poured out on him in the end were twice as much as he had before (Job 42:10, 12).

Because suffering is temporary and may take diverse forms, it is inappropriate to associate a certain kind of suffering as always representing suffering for righteousness' sake. For example, although a believer could suffer financial loss as a result of taking a stand for Christ (as the early Christians did), it would be incorrect to think that being financially stressed and limited **always** represents suffering for righteousness' sake.

Allowed by God, Not Caused by God

Some suffering is allowed by God, but does not come from God. God allows our faith to be tested, and he allows us to experience adversity and affliction because of our obedience to Him. However, he does not always send the adversity. This distinction is important.

If a believer is ostracized at work because he refuses to join his co-workers in telling sexist jokes and forwarding pornographic emails, then one could rightly argue that God is allowing the believer to be tested, but did not inspire the co-workers to do evil. The testing is **allowed by** God, but does not **come from** God.

We can apply the same logic to some financial trials that come our way. God may permit us to be tested by scarcity (for reasons unrelated to the judgment of sin), but he did not send the scarcity. It is not God's will for us to indefinitely have financial lack in our lives; however, it could absolutely be God's will that we are temporarily tested by lack (Hebrews 10:32–34).

To believe in divine financial prosperity does not mean that one will never face financial tests or trials. However, the tests and trials do not change the truthfulness of God's promises or his intentions about his children. Nor should

God's people interpret God's will for their lives by focusing on the tests and trials. In other words, a financial trial does not mean that God wants us to be poor; it could mean that God is using the trial so we will become tested and approved in Him (Romans 16:10).

Suffering is Part of God's Prosperity Plan

What purpose does suffering for the sake of righteousness serve? It prepares us to be better servants:

> 16 So we do not lose heart. Though our outer self is wasting away, our inner self is being renewed day by day.
>
> 17 For this light momentary affliction is preparing for us an eternal weight of glory beyond all comparison,
>
> 18 as we look not to the things that are seen but to the things that are unseen. For the things that are seen are transient, but the things that are unseen are eternal.
>
> 2 Corinthians 4:16–18 (ESV).

> 2 Count it all joy, my brothers, when you meet trials of various kinds,
>
> 3 for you know that the testing of your faith produces steadfastness.
>
> 4 And let steadfastness have its full effect, that you may be perfect and complete, lacking in nothing.
>
> James 1:2–4 (ESV).

The witness of the Apostles is that trials and afflictions for the sake of righteousness improve our faith and make us better for this life and the life that is to come. These kinds of sufferings, therefore, are part of how God causes his Church to **prosper**.

Divine prosperity is more than money. It is God's grace and blessing working in our lives in every way. Though all the promises of God belong to the believer, Jesus Christ in his present-day ministry administrates **how and when** these blessings manifest in our lives. Suffering for doing well is one of the ways in which the Lord positions his Church to receive his best.

The Mystery of Christ's Suffering

PETER REFERS TO A third kind of suffering: the suffering that Christ suffered for us. There is a way in which the Church can emulate the suffering of Christ, and there is a way in which the Church could never imitate his suffering:

> [21] For to this you have been called, because Christ also suffered for you, leaving you an example, so that you might follow in his steps.
>
> [22] He committed no sin, neither was deceit found in his mouth.
>
> [23] When he was reviled, he did not revile in return; when he suffered, he did not threaten, but continued entrusting himself to him who judges justly.
>
> [24] He himself bore our sins in his body on the tree, that we might die to sin and live to righteousness. By his wounds you have been healed.
>
> [25] For you were straying like sheep, but have now returned to the Shepherd and Overseer of your souls.
>
> 1 Peter 2:21–25 (ESV).

Christ left the Church an example to follow in that he led a holy life, did not retaliate when reviled, and bore his unjust suffering with patience and faith. I referred to this kind of suffering in the last chapter. However, in the same passage, Peter refers to a suffering that the believer cannot follow:

> [24] He himself bore our sins in his body on the tree, that we might die to sin and live to righteousness. By his wounds you have been healed.

Only Jesus Christ of Nazareth could be the one to suffer and die on the cross, be raised on the third day, and thus, provide salvation to all men. Moreover, this act of redemption has occurred only once; it is a **finished** work. The Romans continued to crucify men after Jesus had long since ascended. Nevertheless, their sacrifice had no part to play in cleansing men from sin or in reconciling men to God. Therefore, the penalty that Jesus bore on the cross was a suffering that we would not have to endure: he took our place.

I praise God that the Holy Spirit inspired Peter to include the sentence: "By his wounds you have been healed." This is a reference to **physical healing** (see Matthew 8:14–17).

Jesus bore sin on the cross so we may be reconciled to God, become righteous, and live a sanctified life. Jesus was wounded as part of his redemptive suffering so that we may be physically healed.

As noted in chapter 9, the apostle Paul gives additional Spirit-inspired insight into the mystery of the cross:

> [13] Christ redeemed us from the curse of the law by becoming a curse for us—for it is written, "Cursed is everyone who is hanged on a tree"—

The Mystery of Christ's Suffering

¹⁴ so that in Christ Jesus the blessing of Abraham might come to the Gentiles, so that we might receive the promised Spirit through faith.

Galatians 3:13-14 (ESV).

Galatians 3 is talking about Christ being crucified (Galatians 3:1). Christ's crucifixion lifts the curse of the Law and brings the blessing of Abraham. This act of redemption was unique and will never be repeated or duplicated. Christ's sacrifice is a complete and finished work (Hebrews 10:10–14).

Therefore, the logic is simple; if Christ suffered and bore my sins, my sickness and even my poverty, then I do not have to. These types of anguishes do not constitute the suffering God intended for me.

Suffering Due to Satanic Affliction

Peter addresses another type of suffering:

> [8] Be sober-minded; be watchful. Your adversary the devil prowls around like a roaring lion, seeking someone to devour.
>
> [9] Resist him, firm in your faith, knowing that the same kinds of suffering are being experienced by your brotherhood throughout the world.
>
> 1 Peter 5:8–9 (ESV).

The work of the devil brings suffering, and this is the only kind of suffering that Peter instructs the believer to resist. A believer could not, and should not, resist the suffering that comes from being chastened of the Lord–repentance is the only response to that. In addition, a believer cannot stop the suffering that occurs because of doing good and believing God–that kind of suffering is inevitable and should be endured. Although suffering for the sake of righteousness could have a demonic dimension to it in the form of beatings, false imprisonments, and the like, Christians cannot ignore the reproach of the Gospel or dispel suffering for our faith through prayer alone. We can, however, receive God's grace to endure it and finally be victorious over it.

However, the attack of Satan is a peculiar category of suffering. Satan seeks to afflict all people, including Christians, with sickness, disease, tragedy, poverty, and other types of oppression, as part of his activity on the earth (see chapter 10).

Believers can command the devil to stop and he must obey us because of our authority in Christ. There has been much abuse and misleading teaching in this area, but that is no reason for the Church to cede this important aspect of our authority. If there is a satanic power hindering our finances, then only the name of Jesus will overcome it.

Reconciling Prosperity and Suffering

WITHOUT DOUBT, JESUS ENDURED poverty. The Apostles and the early Church suffered deprivation and financial setbacks. So how are we to interpret Paul's teaching on material prosperity in the light of such suffering and poverty? How do we reconcile God's promise of prosperity with the biblical certainty of suffering and struggle?

Rich and Poor Are Relative Concepts

The concepts of wealth and poverty in Scripture are relative and often not aligned to how we use these terms in modern society. People from the West think about wealth and poverty within carefully defined boundaries, whereas the scriptural use of these terms is often broader. Therefore, when the Apostles taught about receiving riches because of giving, for example, they were not necessarily saying that believers who give would find themselves in the top income bracket. Instead, they intended the Church to understand that God wanted them to have abundance. Therefore, the scriptural references to wealth and poverty are **specific**, but they are not usually **equivalent** to how they are used in modern societies.

Unfortunately, the mass media drives the Church's understanding of wealth and poverty though it usually contradicts the biblical view. For example, because an inordinate amount of media coverage of rich celebrities is usually dedicated to **misbehaving** rich celebrities, Christians have a hard time reconciling wealth with holiness.

In the Light of Divine Prosperity, Why Was Jesus Poor?

The life of Jesus illustrates the disparity between the scriptural and secular understanding of wealth and poverty. The Bible says that Jesus Christ was poor (2 Corinthians 8:9). Since 2 Corinthians 8 and 9 are expositions on Christian finances, this reference to the poverty of Christ was primarily, if not exclusively, a financial reference.

The poverty of Christ is also seen in the Gospels. Jesus was a man of modest means who lived plainly. For example, Jesus did not ride in a gold chariot, or travel with a small army for protection. He did not sleep in palaces and associate only with the wealthy. Christ was poor, but his poverty does not invalidate the argument in favor of Christian prosperity for a number of reasons.

First, Jesus' poverty must be understood as relative because the Scriptures also indicate that Jesus was a recipient of a small fortune when he was born. The first thing the Father did was to ensure that Jesus' parents had plenty of money, even as a baby.

Matthew records that the Magi gave the baby Jesus precious and expensive gifts–they did not travel for miles on end across the desert just to give Jesus fifty dollars. The Magi were part of a lineage of Babylonian wise men mentioned in the book of Daniel. In fact, Daniel was promoted as a ruler over them, and some theologians believe it was Daniel who introduced the Magi to the concept of a coming Messiah. Therefore, the Magi had been waiting for centuries for the appearance of the Christ. If they felt that it was their spiritual obligation to come and worship the Christ and bring offerings, then it is likely that the value of their gifts indicated the weight and significance of their beliefs. Although the Scripture does not give a dollar value of the Magi's gifts, it is reasonable to conclude that their offering was a source of wealth for Jesus and his parents.

Furthermore, in his earthly ministry, Jesus was not financially penniless. He received offerings from his followers and had a full-time staff, including a treasurer; this indicates that he had a flow of money. Jesus' mastery of resources was such that he could feed thousands, cover the financial needs of his staff, including paying their taxes, and arrange for transportation and lodging as needed on demand. These are not the actions of a poor person. The Western view of *poor* is a lack of options, financial and otherwise. Poor people are restricted in their ability to pay their bills, pay their taxes, and provide for their families, much less the needs of others. Jesus' earthly life was not consistent with this view of poverty.

The reference to Jesus' poverty in 2 Corinthians 8 contrasts what Jesus had on the earth as opposed to what he had in heaven. It points to the divine condescension of Christ: that Jesus, the greatest king the world has ever known, did not appear with the trappings of wealth and power, but as a meek and lowly prophet.

Perhaps most important, the poverty of Jesus on the earth was redemptive. Paul's point was that Jesus became poor so the Church may become rich. Religious tradition asserts the opposite: that Jesus became poor, and, therefore the Church should be poor as well. This kind of ingrained religious thinking explains why many Christians become upset when they are told that the Bible says they should be rich. However, Jesus' redemptive work was unique: his poverty made us rich (2 Corinthians 8:9).

In addition, a commonly forgotten notion concerns the fact that, although Jesus was poor in his earthly ministry, he is not poor **today:**

> 11 Then I looked, and I heard around the throne and the living creatures and the elders the voice of many angels, numbering myriads of myriads and thousands of thousands,
>
> 12 saying with a loud voice, "Worthy is the Lamb who was slain, to receive **power and wealth** and wisdom and might and honor and glory and blessing!"
>
> Revelation 5:11-12 (ESV).

The One who arose from the dead with all power in heaven and the earth and is seated at the right hand of the Father is far from poor. He inherited wealth from the Father and we are his joint-heirs. Jesus once was poor, but he is not poor anymore!

In the Light of Divine Prosperity, Why Were the Apostles Poor?

The Apostles who led the early Church often experienced suffering, persecution, and deprivation. This included financial hardship and trials. In fact, the two are related: intense persecution often leads to financial loss. So if the Apostles, who have a special status in the Church, suffered these things, does this not mean that the message of prosperity is untrue?

First, I could easily reverse the question: *If God wants his people to be poor, then why was Abraham, David and many others in the Bible rich? In the New Testament, we have record of wealthy and influential Christians. Why did God permit this? And why did God promise such extraordinary abundance in both the Old and New Testaments?*

The answer is that the Christian life is not a binary, black-or-white experience; it is a blended experience. There are highs and lows, and there is the life that occurs in between. Specifically, when we look at the life of the Apostles, we readily acknowledge their hardships and sufferings. However, we have to also acknowledge that the Apostles did not experience hardship and suffering daily. Yes, they had setbacks, but they also experienced victory and abundance as well. For example, the apostle Paul undoubtedly suffered financial distress. Looking at the life of Paul at a high level, we may be tempted to think that he never experienced prosperity. However, Paul describes his financial situation in Philippians 4:

> [10] I rejoiced greatly in the Lord that at last you renewed your concern for me. Indeed, you were concerned, but you had no opportunity to show it.
>
> [11] I am not saying this because I am in need, for I have learned to be content whatever the circumstances.
>
> [12] **I know what it is to be in need, and I know what it is to have plenty.** I have learned the secret of being content in any and every situation, whether well fed or hungry, **whether living in plenty or in want.**
>
> [13] I can do all this through him who gives me strength.
>
> Philippians 4:10–13 (NIV).

Every preacher in America has talked about Paul being in need, but how many talk about Paul having plenty? If we allow Paul to speak for himself, he told the Church at Philippi, "I have been in need [financially] and I have had plenty [financially]." Paul experienced hunger, but he also experienced being well fed. Divine prosperity does not mean that you will **never** experience hunger, or **only** experience being well fed. Divine prosperity is not determined by your moment-to-moment experiences. Divine prosperity is an overall condition; it characterizes a covenant relationship with the Father through Christ. With the hardships he was referring to in Philippians 4, Paul summarized his life this way: "I can do everything through him who gives me strength." **That** is divine prosperity! Note that Paul did not say, *I can do some things through Christ, and if I only had more* *money, I'd be able to do more.* No. Paul said that he could do all things through Christ who strengthens him.

The Apostles learned that true divine prosperity was not determined by how much gold they had stored, or by the influence they had with local politicians. They understood that true prosperity was being connected to the source, Jesus Christ. Paul wrote:

> **[18] I have received full payment and have more than enough. I am amply supplied, now that I have received from Epaphroditus the gifts you sent.** They are a fragrant offering, an acceptable sacrifice, pleasing to God.
>
> [19] And my God will meet all your needs according to the riches of his glory in Christ Jesus.
>
> Philippians 4:18–19 (NIV).

The apostle Paul lived off the Gospel. At times in his ministry, he worked part-time, but he also received offerings from the churches that he founded. Although, for various reasons, the Philippian church was not always consistent in their benevolence, when they sent offerings to Paul, they were generous and abundant. Paul was thanking and commending the Philippians for their support, which "amply" supplied his financial and material needs. They sent an abundant gift, such that Paul wrote that God regarded it as a "fragrant offering" and "an acceptable sacrifice."

This paints a different picture of the apostle Paul. Paul experienced all kinds of hardships, including severe financial deprivations, but those hardships did not define his life or ministry. He also experienced divine prosperity and abundance.

Most important, Paul did not refer to himself as poor. He said of himself, "I can do all things through Christ who strengthens me." This is the language of prosperity, not poverty; this is the language of abundance, not need.

Paul's testimony keeps us balanced. On the one hand, we understand that although Paul experienced financial hardship, Paul was not flat broke. He experienced lack, but he also experienced abundance. This is consistent with the biblical view.

Secondly, Paul advocated moderation. He was content. Paul did not measure success or well-being by the number of the things he possessed. To all intents, Paul was dead to material possessions. If he had them, great, but if he did not have them, he could cope. The secret of his contentment and moderation was that he understood he could do all things through Christ. Therefore, Paul's lifestyle gives the lie to the notion that Christians who believe in divine prosperity are pursuing greed and materialism.

Furthermore, the Scriptures do not say that the Apostles were poor even in the modern understanding of poverty. The Apostles received offerings, regularly gave to the poor, and provided for the needs of their ministerial assistants. The Apostles taught the early Christians to work, to be fiscally responsible and avoid unmanageable debt, and to lead lives of transparent, fiscal integrity.

In the Light of Divine Prosperity, Why Was the Early Church Poor?

The apostle Paul wrote:

> ¹ Now I want you to know, dear brothers and sisters, what God in his kindness has done through the Churches in Macedonia.
>
> ² **They are being tested by many troubles, and they are very poor.** But they are also filled with abundant joy, which has overflowed in rich generosity.
>
> ³ For I can testify that they gave not only what they could afford, but far more. And they did it of their own free will.
>
> 2 Corinthians 8:1–3 (NLT).

In this passage, Paul reveals that the Christians in Macedonia were going through intense sufferings and were experiencing deep poverty, although we do not know all the details. Despite their financial situation, the Macedonians freely gave to Paul's relief fund for the churches in Judea, donating even beyond what they were able. Paul is calling attention to the Macedonian situation trying to spur the Corinthians to finish the benevolence that they had started. In doing so, Paul reminds the Corinthians of a promise that applied to the Macedonian Christians as well:

> ⁶ Remember this: Whoever sows sparingly will also reap sparingly, and whoever sows generously will also reap generously.
>
> ⁷ Each of you should give what you have decided in your heart to give, not reluctantly or under compulsion, for God loves a cheerful giver.

Foundations of Divine Prosperity

> ⁸ And God is able to bless you abundantly, so that in all things at all times, having all that you need, you will abound in every good work.
>
> 2 Corinthians 9:6–8 (NIV).

Paul taught the churches about giving and receiving and the Macedonians were eager to give because they believed these messages about prosperity. They loved their brethren in Jerusalem and wanted to help them; however, they also understood that the financial seeds they sowed would reap a financial harvest. As Paul taught them, the Macedonian Christians understood that if they sowed sacrificially, generously, and with a sincere desire to help others, then they could expect that God would cause them to reap generously. Because of their trust in this spiritual reality, the Macedonian Christians were not dismayed by their financial problems. They gave in spite of their poverty, because they understood that they would eventually receive the promise of prosperity.

This passage reiterates how the biblical truth of suffering and the biblical truth of divine prosperity co-exist. Suffering is a circumstance and prosperity is a covenant promise; the two are not incompatible.

Some strenuously argue that *prosperity teaching* does not work in emergent countries. This is nonsense. There is no biblical precedent of God being limited by a person's home address. The apostle Paul does not imply that the Macedonian Christians were predestined to be financially impoverished for all time, or that there was a geographic limitation to God's promises. Paul held up their giving, and the promises attached to their giving, as an incentive for the Corinthians. Whoever sows generously will reap generously. This is true for the Macedonian or the Corinthian, for those in great need financially, or those overflowing with abundance. Indeed, it is through giving that the poor can overcome their poverty and experience God's abundance.

Summary on Suffering

THE BIBLICAL DOCTRINE OF suffering is broad and deep. Properly understood, it is a beautiful doctrine, fitting perfectly into the mosaic of redemption. To believe in divine prosperity is not to set aside the reality of suffering. Although the Church has been given unique advantages in this life, our election in Christ does not make us exempt from trial, tribulation, or suffering. Believers must be careful to guard their hearts, so when trials do come, they do not become bitter or resentful and fall away from the faith.

The many categories of suffering mean that believers are responsible for discovering the cause of trials in their lives. There are many reasons that Christians may suffer financially. If Christians refuse to work and develop marketable skills through education, they will suffer the consequences of their disobedience and laziness. If Christians are constantly running up debts that they cannot pay and wantonly overspending, then they are positioning themselves for God's judgment or chastisement. In addition, there are occasions when believers may suffer financial setbacks because of their faith, perhaps being unfairly overlooked for a promotion or a raise because of the evil intent of a boss or co-worker. Besides this, Satan can block a believer's prosperity as well.

The good news is that there is no kind of suffering that, in itself, places us beyond the reach of our heavenly Father and the good promises of his sure Word. With finances, if I am suffering because of disobedience, then I can know that, if I repent, God will restore me and use the experience of that affliction to make me better. If I am suffering for doing good, I can be joyful that *trouble doesn't last always*, and though weeping may endure for a night, joy will come in the morning. Furthermore, I can know that suffering for the sake of righteousness is working an exceeding weight of glory in me.

If I am suffering financially because of the attack of Satan, I can know that I have authority in Christ, and that in Christ I have been raised far above "all principalities and powers, and rulers of this present darkness," and, therefore, if I resist Satan, he must flee.

Enduring delay is also a form of suffering. Christians should not think that they will always receive instant, automatic answers to their prayers, though prosperity belongs to them. Therefore, we should not be discouraged by suffering and delay. Living in divine prosperity is part of a lifestyle of faith that takes effort and involves struggle. It takes time to learn how to pray about financial things not with covetousness, but with patience and perseverance. There are no shortcuts, and there is nothing quick about learning how to live out the authentic, biblical message of prosperity. Even so, developing mastery in these areas is worth the effort. When we do receive our prosperity, we can join the apostle Paul in saying, "Indeed, I have all and abound" (Philippians 4:18 NKJV).

PART 7
PROSPERITY IS CONDITIONAL

Preconditions of Prosperity

DIVINE PROSPERITY IS A conditional blessing. For example, when Paul writes that God is able to make all grace abound to us for us to continually prosper, that marvelous promise is preceded by the condition we give generously.

The motif of conditional promises in the Bible does not suggest that believers can earn God's blessing. Divine preconditions merely reflect the order of God that is already apparent in creation. For example, sowing is a precondition to reaping, both spiritually and naturally. That God has revealed what the preconditions are to prospering assures the believer that he indeed wants his children to prosper by being obedient. The challenge before every Christian is to learn God's ways and to apply them in everyday life. Not in a legalistic sense, instead with the understanding that following scriptural principles respects God's order and will achieve scriptural results.

The Necessity of Faith

Faith is one of the principal requirements to receive from God. Because faith itself is the gift of God, no man can take credit for believing. However, it is also true that God has established that the act of believing is **man's** choice and continuing responsibility. As the Scriptures say, "the just shall live by faith."

Modern Christians often use the term, *faith* to refer to the body of beliefs that represent Christian orthodoxy, for example, saying, *I am of the Christian faith*. However, Scripture also defines faith as "the **substance** of things hoped for" (Hebrews 11:1), that is, the divine material and platform that God gives the Church to trust Him and manifest his promises. This is the faith Jesus spoke of when he talked about using our faith to move mountains (Mark 11).

Although there are intersecting conditions related to receiving from God, faith is a principal requirement, so it is crucial to understand what faith is and how it works. A person may be of the Christian faith and still lack Bible faith or be unaware that their faith should be put to work. For example, Jesus' disciples believed that Jesus was the Messiah (that is they had faith in a generic sense), but Jesus more than once rebuked them for having little faith. In addition, Jesus frequently asked supplicants if they had faith for what they were asking and he often told those who had been healed and delivered that it was their faith that saved them.

Employing Bible faith releases the power of God and God expects his people to learn how to live by faith.

Let us consider what Jesus said about this kind of Bible faith:

> [23] For assuredly, I say to you, whoever says to this mountain, 'Be removed and be cast into the sea,' and does not doubt

Preconditions of Prosperity

> in his heart, but believes that those things he says will be done, he will have whatever he says.
>
> ²⁴ Therefore I say to you, whatever things you ask when you pray, believe that you receive them, and you will have them.
>
> ²⁵ And whenever you stand praying, if you have anything against anyone, forgive him, that your Father in heaven may also forgive you your trespasses.
>
> Mark 11:23–25 (NKJV)

Jesus taught believers could move mountains (a reference to the everyday problems Christians encounter) by using their faith. This faith operates in a straightforward manner:

- All things for which we pray and ask, we must believe that we receive them (first), and then we shall have them (after we have believed)

- Faith is of the heart, which is our spirit. True Bible faith is to believe God in the heart, not necessarily with the intellect. Conversely, doubt–that negates faith–also manifests in the heart.

- Faith is expressed by **saying.** Jesus said, "whoever **says** to this mountain." We release faith by speaking words of faith.

- Jesus identified two hindrances to faith (and, therefore, answered prayer): doubt and withholding forgiveness. This means that our attitude and behavior can cancel our faith and prevent our prayers from being answered.

- The proof of our faith is for us to **believe** that what we say will come to pass **before we see it come it pass.**

Faith comes by hearing the Word of God (Romans 10:17) and the importance of faith is underscored by the calamitous effect of doubt on our spiritual progress. As noted above, Jesus said that doubt would negate our faith (and implied lack of forgiveness would as well). In Mark 6, the offense and unbelief of the people limited Christ from doing mighty works of healing and deliverance as he typically did, and the Scripture records that Jesus actually marveled at their unbelief. The writer of Hebrews explains that the generation of the Exodus did not enter into the Promised Land because of their unbelief:

> ² For indeed the gospel was preached to us as well as to them; **but the word which they heard did not profit them, not being mixed with faith in those who heard it.**
>
> Hebrews 4:2 (NKJV)

Although God promised Israel a land of milk of honey, that generation failed to receive it because they lacked faith. Doubt and unbelief can cause you to lose your prosperity though it belongs to you in Christ!

Prosperity Is a Lifestyle

The Apostles taught that believers receive manifestations to their prayers through faith and patience or endurance (Hebrews 10). The qualification of patient endurance and perseverance indicate that the blessings of God, including material blessings like healing and financial prosperity, are not automatic and typically are not instantaneous. The believer needs to stand and persevere in faith before they receive what has been promised.

There have been Christians who heard a message of divine prosperity, began to pray for things, and when their answers did not come as quickly as expected, they became discouraged and lost hope. They became bitter and resentful at those who preach prosperity, and began to give negative testimony. It is heartbreaking to read the blogs and commentary of Christians who have been disappointed by the so-called *health and wealth message*. Although my heart goes out to any child of God who has been hurt and offended, the fact is, God's promises of prosperity are not **magic**. The promises of God about finances do not work independently of, or differently from, the other promises in the Bible. If believers in the Bible had to wait patiently for the manifestations of God's promises, believers today will have to wait patiently as well. If believers in the Bible had to learn how to pray in faith and prevail in prayer, then we will have to learn how to do so as well. Importantly, Christians should not think that they can operate in faith perfectly at the outset any more than they should think a toddler can learn to walk without falling.

There are preachers who preach poorly. However, the parable of the Sower (Matthew 8) teaches us that failure to receive the promises of the Word is primarily a failure of hearing and attitude, not a failure of preaching. Bearing fruit is not easy, and failure, in any circumstance, is a real possibility. Although it can be difficult to bounce back from a spiritual disappointment, one can get back on track. Indeed, the parable of the Sower shows us how to troubleshoot spiritual failures in our lives so we can do better next time.

Living by faith also involves learning how to endure painful trials, fiery afflictions, and satanic pressure to receive the manifestation of divine promises. The suffering is not merely the content of the suffering–the mistreatment, the reproach, the confiscation of prosperity, the physical pain and illness–but it is also the temptation to let go of faith in the face of these struggles. Indeed, the reason that the afflictions come is to get the believer to **stop** believing and let go of their faith. The writer of Hebrews speaks to this in Hebrews 10:32–38. The struggle to persevere, as the Hebrew Christians were doing, is the struggle that every Christian is called to endure.

PART 8
EPILOGUE

Super Prosperity

DIVINE PROSPERITY IS NOT defined by things, but by a connection to Jesus Christ. Jesus is the administrator of the blessing of Abraham to those who trust him, and, therefore, he is the one who ensures that our needs are met according to his riches in glory. Although we may not know how the Lord will meet our needs, we can trust that he will do so perfectly and abundantly.

It is unfortunate that some prominent prosperity teaching is preoccupied with the accumulation of things. Although things are an undeniable component of divine prosperity, and seeing people do well inspires others to do well themselves, the emphasis on conspicuous consumption has obscured the beauty of the biblical promises of prosperity.

The genius of God's prosperity plan is its minimalist and portable quality. Believers do not need an armored truck following them wherever they go to get their needs met. Any child of God can tap into God's unlimited, heavenly resources merely by believing Christ will faithfully provide what is needed. Therefore, God's promises of abundant provision do not necessarily translate into multiplied millions in the bank. God's provision is beyond the human standards of prosperity; therefore, even in the face of affliction and lack, the Church may confidently declare her needs met by Christ Jesus. Whether hungry or well fed, rich or poor, we can know that we can do all things through Christ who strengthens us. This is **super prosperity.**

Super prosperity may take the form of having lots of money, much the way God made Abraham, Joseph, and Daniel wealthy. However, it could also be having cool water flow from rocks in the desert, or a raven to feed you meat during a time of famine. **Super prosperity is having what you need when you need it, despite your circumstances.**

Understanding our portion and place in God enhances our ability to flow in this divine prosperity. As we seek first God's kingdom, and understand where the Lord wants us to be and what he wants us to do, then we will recognize the portion of our inheritance, and become more effective at receiving divine prosperity.

Super prosperity is entirely consistent with an orthodox understanding of Scripture. It acknowledges the reality of suffering, the likelihood of delays, and the necessity of standing patiently in faith. It is not a get-rich-quick scheme, but a lifestyle of faith tempered by moderation, bounded by holiness and marked by divine favor and supernatural increase.

If you are called to be a wife and mother, the Lord wants to bless you in your calling beyond your wildest imagination. I have no idea what that looks like for you, but I do know that it includes everything you need to be the best wife and mother that you can be, and to be a blessing to the world around you.

If you are called into the ministry, then provision has been made for you to have everything you need to execute your ministry. This may not translate into your ministry owning a fleet of jets and gleaming offices settled on a rolling campus. However, whatever your portion, it will be sweet and satisfying to your soul and will enable you to do what you never thought you could do for God.

If you are called to the business world, know that there is no limit to the prosperity that God can give you if you walk uprightly before him. You may not become the richest man in the world, or even make the annual *Forbes'* list of wealthy individuals, but God will give you all that you need to succeed if you trust Him.

It is my prayer that you will embrace your calling, and seek to possess your inheritance in Christ, so you may prosper in all things and do great things for the kingdom of God.

PART 9
APPENDIX

Appendix

Use of Bible Versions

English-speaking people have been blessed to have many various translations of the Scripture. The wording of a particular translation can bring out the meaning of a passage in innovative and thought-provoking ways that enhance our understanding. Therefore, I have used various translations liberally throughout this book.

All the versions listed below can be accessed online at biblegateway.com, biblestudytools.com, and bible.org. I encourage you to use these tools to look up the cited Scripture references.

Bible References

The abbreviations for biblical translations used in this book are:

- Amplified—Amplified Bible
- CEV—Contemporary English Version
- ESV—English Standard Version
- KJV—King James Version
- MSG—The Message Bible
- NAS—New American Standard Bible
- NCV—New Century Version
- NET—New English Translation
- NIV—New International Version
- NLT—New Living Translation
- NKJV—New King James Version
- YLT—Young's Literal Translation

Scripture references in boldface indicate my emphasis, which does not appear in the original text.

Appendix

Copyright Information

- Scripture marked as (Amplified) are taken from the Amplified® Bible. Copyright © 1954, 1958, 1962, 1964, 1965, 1987 by The Lockman Foundation. Used by permission. (www.Lockman.org)

- Scriptures marked (CEV) are taken from the Contemporary English Version. Copyright © 1995 by American Bible Society. Used by permission.

- Scripture quotations marked (ESV) are from The Holy Bible, English Standard Version® (ESV®), copyright © 2001 by Crossway, a publishing ministry of Good News Publishers. Used by permission. All rights reserved.

- Scripture quotations marked (KJV) are taken from the King James Version of the Holy Bible, public domain.

- Scripture quotations marked (MSG) are taken from The Message. Copyright 1993, 1994, 1995, 1996, 2000, 2001, 2002. Used by permission of NavPress Publishing Group.

- Scripture quotations marked (NASB) are taken from the NEW AMERICAN STANDARD BIBLE®. Copyright © 1960, 1962, 1963, 1968, 1971, 1972, 1973, 1975, 1977, 1995 by The Lockman Foundation. Used by permission.

- Scripture quotations marked (NCV) are taken from the New Century Version®. Copyright © 2005 by Thomas Nelson, Inc. Used by permission. All rights reserved.

- Scripture quoted by permission. Quotations designated (NET) are from the NET Bible® copyright ©1996–2006 by Biblical Studies Press, L.L.C. http://bible.org All rights reserved.

- Scripture quotations marked (NIV) are taken from the Holy Bible, New International Version®, NIV®. Copyright ©1973, 1978, 1984 by Biblica, Inc.™ Used by permission of Zondervan. All rights reserved worldwide.

- Scripture quotations marked (NKJV) are taken from the New King James Version®. Copyright © 1982 by Thomas Nelson, Inc. Used by permission. All rights reserved.
- Scripture quotations marked (NLT) are taken from the Holy Bible, New Living Translation, copyright © 1996, 2004, 2007 by Tyndale House Foundation. Used by permission of Tyndale House Publishers, Inc., Carol Stream, Illinois 60188. All rights reserved.
- Scripture quotations marked (YLT) are taken from Young's Literal Translation of the Holy Bible, public domain.

Appendix

Works Cited

Chant, Ken. *Faith Dynamics*. Ramona, CA: Vision Publishing, 1989.

Hagin, Kenneth E. *Man On Three Dimensions*. Tulsa, OK: RHEMA Bible Church, 1991.

Merriam-Webster, Incorporated. *Merriam-Webster's Collegiate Dictionary, Eleventh Edition*. Springfield, Massachusetts: Merriam-Webster Incorporated, 2003.

Snell, Jay. *What've They Done With Abraham's Blessings?* Vol. 1. Livingston, Texas: Jay Snell Evangelistic Association, 1989.

Vines, W.E. *Vine's Expository Dictionary of New Testament Words*. 1940.

Appendix

Endnotes

1. Some believe John's opening to Gaius was merely a greeting. Whether it was a salutation does not diminish the fact that it was inspired by the Holy Spirit and has significance in understanding God's will for believers.
2. Vine, W.E. "Prosper." Vine's Expository Dictionary of New Testament Words. 1940.
3. "Prosperity." Merriam-Webster Collegiate Dictionary. 2009. Print.
4. The translated Greek word for *soul* is psyche; the Greek word for *spirit* is pneuma. Although these words are close in meaning, psyche refers to "the seat of the feelings, desires, affections, aversion"; spirit refers to "the vital principle by which the body is animated." Blue Letter Bible, "Dictionary and Word Search for psyche (Strong's 5590)." Blue Letter Bible, 1996–2008. 25 Oct 2008. Blue Letter Bible, "Dictionary and Word Search for pneuma (Strong's 4151)." Blue Letter Bible, 1996–2008. 25 Oct 2008.
5. Bible scholars have commented on the distinction between *soul* and *spirit*: "The language of Hebrews 4:12 suggests the extreme difficulty of distinguishing between the soul and the spirit, like in their nature and in their activities. Generally speaking, the spirit is the higher, the soul the lower element. The spirit may be recognized as the life principle bestowed on man by God, the soul as the resulting life constituted in the individual, the body being the material organism animated by soul and spirit." Taken from, Vine, W. E. "Soul," Vine's Expository Dictionary of New Testament Words. Blue Letter Bible, 1940. 1 Apr 2007. 25 Oct 2008.
6. (Hagin, 1991, 6–7)
7. Blue Letter Bible. "Dictionary and Word Search for *hagah* (Strong's 1897)." Blue Letter Bible, 1996–2010. 23 Dec 2010. http:// www.blueletterbible.org/lang/lexicon/lexicon.cfm? Strongs=H1897&t=KJV
8. "Imagine." Merriam-Webster Collegiate Dictionary. 2009. Print.

9. Generally, my references to "man" refer to men and women. Often, my use of "Adam" refers to both Adam and Eve, because they were co-heirs of creation and considered by God to be one flesh.
10. Vine, W. E. "Inherit, Inheritance." Vine's Expository Dictionary of New Testament Words. 1940.
11. We can see from these Scriptures that the words *inheritance*, *possession*, *blessing*, and *promise* are used interchangeably. In this book, we use those terms interchangeably as well.
12. (Snell, 1989, 2–11).
13. Although this explanation of the curse of the Law is not new to Christian thought, the phrase *the curse of the Law is poverty, sickness, and spiritual death* is a phrase that I first heard from Dr. Kenneth E. Hagin.
14. Blue Letter Bible. "Dictionary and Word Search for tēreō (Strong's 5083)." Blue Letter Bible. 1996–2011. 8 Apr 2011. < http:// www.blueletterbible.org/lang/lexicon/lexicon.cfm? Strongs=G5083&t=KJV >
15. (Chant, 1989, 22).
16. "Content." Blue Letter Bible. "Dictionary and Word Search for arke (Strong's 714)." Blue Letter Bible, 1996–2010. 30 Dec 2010. http:// www.blueletterbible.org/lang/lexicon/lexicon.cfm?Strongs=G714&t=NIV